LIFE IS EASY

people make it hard

FREE the past, present & future you

ROBERT NETZEL AND PATTY SNEED

Copyright © 2023 Robert Netzel and Patty Sneed

Published by CaryPress International Books

www.CaryPress.com

All rights reserved. No part of this publication may be reproduced, distributed, or transmitted in any form or by any means, including photocopying, recording, or other electronic or mechanical methods, without the prior written permission of the publisher, except in the case of brief quotations embodied in critical reviews and certain other noncommercial uses permitted by copyright law.

A psychological opinion about the human condition and the complexities of effective communication; inspired by some of the great minds from yesterday.

This book contains both content and workbook sections that could seem, at times, challenging. Hopefully, as you move through the book slowly, steadily, and with patience, personal clarity will become visible. Most likely, you will feel a need to re-read certain sentences, paragraphs, or chapters before there are true light bulb moments. That is its purpose! We want you to utilize this book as a tool in understanding the journey we call life. To identify meaningful concepts, connections, and thought processes that bring you joy. Your journey is unique, and we believe in freeing the past, present, and future you.

CONTENTS

Chapter 1 – Circumstances and Outcomes 1

Chapter 2 – Why – Assigned without Consent 22

Chapter 3 – Who – Established through Identity 40

Chapter 4 – What – Reinforced by Approval 48

Chapter 5 – How – Means to an End 58

Chapter 6 – When – Navigating your Opportunities 67

Chapter 7 – Peace and Happiness 76

References 85

Patty's Note

We are all born in _(blank)_ likeness, so we all have something to contribute to this crazy world, and that doesn't mean something huge; it just means something. Notice I didn't say small because there's no way to categorize our impact. What's profound to one of us is trivial to the next and vice versa. Our goal is to live in the present. There's no deadline to work on ourselves. Who are we to judge?

NO ONE is here without a purpose… we simply need to find _ours_. This isn't a rah-rah book; it's a workbook, and Sal & I are not famous or successful people sharing some grandiose story. We are brother and sister raised in a traditional family in the Midwest, in the 1970s and 80s, where faith, family, and fellowship mattered above all else. We want to give people everywhere a chance to intimately see the simple truth of their lives based on what we've seen and learned over our combined perspectives of 100+ years of living. Life's not hard; it's people that make it so.

So, what if you, too, could better understand yourself in order to understand others? Love others. We'll all dive to different depths to do so, which is totally cool. Know this - we struggle alone a lot more than we were designed to. So go in peace … ☺ My brother says I have an annoying tendency to sound like I'm giving a sermon and I promise I'm not, but I can't help it and you'll find out why in this workbook! ☺ People don't change…

They just get better!

CHAPTER 1

Circumstances and Outcomes

It never ceases to amaze me (Sal, here) how you can end up on the right path and with the right people, not by any degree of perfection in you, just by a matter of trying. There is no one perfect path in life, and we will all make mistakes along the way. But if we keep trying, we will eventually find our way to where we are meant to be. The people we meet in life are there for a reason. They may teach us something, help us grow, or make our lives more enjoyable. Even if we only meet someone briefly, they can still have a lasting impact on us.

I'm a big believer in giving it your best and seeing how your efforts impact your life and the lives around you. Of course, be ready to alter your course if your efforts aren't proving helpful in the long run. I remember one trip in particular when several synchronicities made themselves apparent to me and my sister Patty.

I'll share some of these with you and, don't worry, Patty will jump in with her own pearls of wisdom in a bit. I want to share part of my life with you here before diving into this story's philosophy. It is my hope that you will be enriched and inspired.

> "There is an *I* in team - But not credit." rjn

Covid was still in full swing in the fall of 2020. I was glad to be able to travel again, going from my home state of North Carolina to visit Patty and her family in Michigan. I breezed through the empty airports, mask firmly under my chin, and outlook positive. Patty's son, Bobby; was there early to pick me up. He's a great kid. He caught me up on the goings-on in his life as we drove to Patty's. I felt happy despite the overcast sky. One thing I love about where I live is the abundance of heat and sunshine. Can't beat it.

I was lucky to have spent a little time with my sister about a month before. We had gotten together for another family member's 55th birthday—what a fun time! You know those family events where things just work out the way they are supposed to, even imperfectly? That weekend of the birthday it seemed many people were curious about themselves, why they did the things they did, and why they held their own biases, often without knowing it. The personality assessment du jour was the Enneagram. Now, I won't bog you down with it too much, but basically, it is a powerful and ancient tool that helps people label themselves (fears, motivations, patterns of behavior changes when faced with stimuli, etc.) for the purpose of healing and moving into the healthy level within their personality type. It's psychology! And I loved it.

But with every change humans encounter, some conflict can arise. This is natural and part of growth as we shed old, limiting beliefs and move into higher realms of enlightenment, humility, and, ultimately, love.

But I digress. Truth be told, I was excited to be in Michigan to see Patty again. We'd been having intense conversations about life and, more importantly, how we live. We easily agreed that everyone has their own way of navigating life's many moments. All these very different attitudes, actions, and reactions can seem random, even chaotic, without a framework through which to see them. I wanted to share with Patty how I've discovered how to understand people and more wisely interpret situations more deeply. Over the years, I've learned that life will always present us with circumstances that are less than ideal, but we humans can influence the outcomes. This and other truths helped me in my darkest times, chief among them being when my dear wife was fighting for survival a decade earlier.

One thing I like about visiting Patty is that she so effortlessly makes things relaxing and inviting. She has a way of making people feel welcome, but in the same way, she can create uncomfortable environments for others. Me, I go along to get along and enjoy interesting people and the stories they share. Together, we make a pretty good team. The night of my arrival was no different.

LIFE IS EASY

I landed, rode home with Bobby, settled, and bam—it was dinner time. Dinner was prepared by my brother-in-law. He is a wonderful cook who puts more time and energy into his sauces than his golf swing. Patty and Jeff are tremendous hosts. They make you feel welcome and at home when around. So, it was not surprising when Patty told me she was having a guest over, her designer friend. My sister is always decorating. Maybe this–Maybe that. *Jeff, we need to update,* etc. But again, I love meeting new people and learning about their perspectives.

Vodka was her name, and she was intriguing to say the least. Dinner was wonderful and as usual, Patty brought it all together with WHY I was there and WHAT we were about to embark on. Great food, a dessert, and a cocktail to wind the night down. We had an early morning, a morning that would keep us in our PJs and sweats until noon and beyond.

Some say I have a little philosopher in me, while others say, "Watch out, that guy can get on a soap box." I do not see it that way… to me, they are my thoughts, and I find enrichment in sharing and being shared with others. One thing about me is that I'm usually on the quiet side. So, when I do share, it takes most by surprise and doesn't fit the expectations they have placed on me. That next morning, Patty and I started by sharing a coffee by the fire, talking about so many things until I utilized an opening to inject my idea of why I believe people are who they are and do not change after they are twenty-one.

Patty was interested, so I drew a simple drawing of my thoughts (picture of the graph). This is where I will let Patty take over the narrative/story. Get ready, though; whereas I am reserved, she is a whirlwind, and I will bet that you can feel her vivacious energy jumping off the next few pages. You're going to love it.

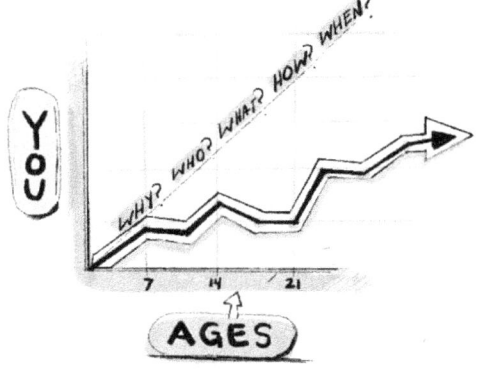

Seeeeeeeeee… I (Patty) have a smile ear to ear, gleaming with the deepest understanding as I respond to what Sal shared with you. That's it. The yin and the yang. Sometimes he says it, and I can elaborate. Sometimes I say it, and after he smirks, really laughs, giggles, and shakes his head back and forth, *he* elaborates.

This is it. We get each other. Why is that? How the heck do we gel? And… here's another kicker… we're married to similar people! We're in the right marriages. They're good at the core. Solid. Definitely right.

Of course, I have to add to what my little brother said, but he's pinned it–the ole tail on the donkey. (Do they say that anymore, or is that a faux pas somehow now?) I don't get all that stuff. It's history. Kinda like the many pieces of drafting paper Sal threw away after four days of pretty solid brainstorming. I asked him, *where are they?* He said, *I condensed them*. TO ONE PAGE. All that work fits into ONE PAGE! Not in my mind. That's men, though. And that's Sal, he falls into that category, *I know what I mean. I don't need to go over it again*. I got it. And like Sal says so well… *Men are a knuckle-dragging species, just tell us what to do.*

Back to the topic at hand, I make assumptions based on being the oldest. The one who everyone for the majority of my first 21 years followed. I was #1 and the world revolved around me; but did it? I have a sister who is 11 months younger than me. And a brother a year after that and another one a year after that. Four of us in four years. My mom was a born caregiver. She was one of seven. A nurse to everyone who needed care. I learned a lot from watching her.

I knew she had tremendous wisdom stored in her mind through decades of living, loving, and losing those she loved, so I started to ask her the questions that are part of this chapter. We didn't finish. It exhausted her. Or should I say, my asking her, exhausted her. And like my exceptionally wise younger brother says… you made it about you. He was right again. Why can't I take the answer for what it is? Why do I need to probe? My curious nature has never been squelched before. And I've always prided myself on my perspective, but I miss the boat sometimes.

But that's the beauty or the shackles of being number ONE in the family. The sun rises and sets on you. We tend to be idealistic; I think. Follow me where I go (by John Denver). Yup, when we're not standing at 10,000 feet, we tend to get caught in the weeds. Do you know who's always got a bird's eye view? The big fella. That's how Sal refers to God.

And that's where we often struggle … when things don't go *our* way based on *our* preferred circumstances like my first 21 years of roses and lollipops. I'm not that naive. I get it… *now*, I was pretty far in life when I got knocked off my horse. Not everyone's born into a family grounded in faith, in the Midwest where 2 natural parents are striving to help others, as well as their careers.

Our father was a music teacher. Our mother was a nurse. He wasn't any teacher but *the guy* who could put on a production and carry his career into the church and onto the stage. Teach others, regardless of age, and bring any event to life… A wedding. A funeral. A Christmas party. A humdrum, rainy, Friday afternoon in the classroom before a weekend with no plans. The "what are we gunna do tonight" Fridays after a torturous week in 11th grade! Hilarious, isn't it? Here again… our book. What would the kid do who was faced with this? And there's no kid in school regardless of where he or she lives, whether 1970 or 2022, that doesn't have this quandary every once in a while.

OK, where was I? Oh, the life of a grandmama. ☺ It's magnificent. That's not the point of this section, but it brings me such joy that I want you to feel it, too. But really, I love being a mom. I love having siblings. I was the oldest of 6 and never suffered because of them.

They brought me joy for the most part, like most people bring me joy… for the most part. I remember and openly celebrate those days before the invention of social media. You may or may not remember, too. Social media, like most things, can be devious. It tends to feed on the human ego's need to feel something. Life with five siblings teaches you that you're one of many and not everyone feels the same way at the same time.

Sal was not one of the first 4 born in 4 years. He came along 3 years after #4. Talk about a bird's eye view. From his perch in the nest looking down and all around at the endless activity, I guess he decided to be quiet. When I was 18 and off to college, he was **12. TWELVE! That's only 7th grade**. No *wonder* he's always so full of material. And I might add that he was and still is damn funny. His dry humor. His timing. His candor. His caring nature. He was taught by watching a bunch of goodie-two-shoes "gone wild" in the center of Iowa where the corn grows tall, and the sky is basically blue all summer. Well—until the Jerry Lewis Telethon that took place on Labor Day weekend. Then the first day of school, is that right? I can't remember now. I do know I had a new outfit, that's for sure. And I felt pretty wearing it.

I have to give credit to Mom. Our mother was a miracle worker. That new outfit was usually handmade, or I always remember saying homemade. Today, that love and care would make the outfit a boutique item, but back then, it wasn't a designer thing and it was probably dorky. NOT TO ME, however! I loved clothes. Going to the fabric store and selecting new material for an outfit or 2 or 5. How in the world did that woman get it all done? She worked full-time as a nurse. Baked fresh bread…, which made the ole Wonder bread a treat. Sometimes, we even removed the crust, rolled the cottony white substance into a flat disc, and played communion in the family room beside our two couches. Kneeling at the coffee table while one of my brothers stood on the hearth playing priest. No one ended up being one, however.

> "Bread is the symbol of the home and family."

Okay, she made the bread we ate, which, by the way, was the absolute best toast. She did all our laundry, cooked every meal, and had it on the table by 5:30 p.m. Monday through Thursday. Friday was all about school activities as we got older. When we were young, I don't remember that evening being different from any other. I remember Saturday night was for adults, so we often stayed home with a babysitter. Sunday was chili or popcorn and Mutual of Omaha's Wild Kingdom followed by the weekly Wonderful World of Disney movie. She took the night off. For goodness' sake, she deserved it. Why did it take us 40 years to appreciate her never-ending duties?

And now we're trying to figure it all out. There's almost a crime in waiting so long. Why? Well, it's not in everyone's DNA to be that curious. Or that reflective. That taskmaster taught us to love our families in the same fashion. To do things for them. To put them first. To love and respect through duty. Sal & I have time to do so in our lives of abundance. To us, it's a lot more fun than sitting on our backsides, scrolling through social media. Yup… rather than being born in 1964 and 1971, we would've fit right in by being born in 1944 and 1951.

So, down the rabbit hole, I go. And this is how we spent 4 days organizing our book 2 and a half years ago. There's sooooooo much to remember and give credit to, so much to pay attention to and dissect. And no one I'd rather do it with than Sal.

During this deep dive into our past (Sal again) and the many ways it shaped us today, I put in the work, using examples of direct interaction, awards, coaches, siblings, friends, work, and school… up to when I turned 21. I wracked my brain, remembering how I perceived Mom and Dad, how they morphed in and out of roles when dealing with people, grandparents, and jobs. It was like an incredible puzzle, uncovering their relationship and how they perceived each one of their children. All that valuable effort was not only to discover how I got to a place where most could recognize me as I am today but to truly understand who or what I was.

It is my hope that you will take your own journey into yourself, your background, your influences, and your current state of being as you read this book, unlocking questions regarding your *Why, Who, What, How, and When*.

Looking Within to See Better Around Us

If circumstances control man and man dictates outcomes, then PEACE rests at the corner of self-awareness and self-acceptance.

There are many things we (Sal and Patty) agree on and the one that has impacted our lives probably the most is the concept that "Circumstances control man–man dictates outcomes." Sounds so simple, right? Something happens to us, and we create the outcome that we want, to the best of our ability. Let's stop and consider the flow of these words.

Circumstances are the conditions or the ways in which things happen to us. Circumstances are fickle, unpredictable, and often out of our control. They come paired with an event (something that happens), and they will always produce an outcome (a result). The danger here is when we start to tie circumstances and outcomes together automatically without questioning the connection and without understanding that we can exert our will and begin to create different, new, and preferred outcomes.

Here's an example. We may have a neutral event, such as going to the gas station to put fuel in our car. That's a fairly standard activity in most people's lives. It can remain neutral, become positive, or drop into something negative. Let's say we see a friend who is also there at the same time, someone we care about and have been meaning to reconnect with. We share a friendly conversation. The outcome is that our mood is elevated, and we receive a hit of dopamine to the brain. We were suddenly so glad we went to the gas station that day. We can't wait to get home and share this happy energy with our spouse. Our entire focus is on the happy outcome. As a result, at least for the next several minutes or hours, we will continue to look for positive interpretations of events happening around us.

The event was going to the gas station. The circumstance (condition) was a positive encounter with a fellow human being. The outcome was a hit of positive chemicals in the brain and a feeling of joy. But the opposite can also be true. It could be raining heavily, and a gust of wind sends a splatter of cold water on you as you are pumping gas. Same event, pumping gas, but in different circumstance or condition. We may leave feeling grumpy, or that life is out of control (outcome). That will influence how we interpret events that happen after we leave. If we are met with several more circumstances that are not within our comfort zone, preferences, or preconceived ideas of how the day should unfold or how people should be treating us, we can easily spiral downward. If left on this path, it will start to impact those around us in negative ways and become increasingly hard to climb out of.

We've noticed that some people seem to have an easier time focusing on getting the outcome they want. Maybe when the rain dumps cold water on them, they get in their car and listen to their favorite song, or they pick up the phone and call that friend they've been meaning to reconnect with. They take an action step for a better outcome.

Have you ever noticed that some people seem to stay within a realm of positivity while others struggle? Some people inherently focus on the big picture and are inspired while others see the many weeds and get lost in them. Some people defy their circumstances and mold life to their wishes while others in the same event and circumstance seem to sit down and surrender. These choices and responses to life are a normal part of the human experience and in adulthood, these patterns are fairly well established.

Usually, as adults, we may recognize the way *we* are and the way other people are; but we don't quite know why and we surely do not dig deeper. We (Sal and Patty) used to be that way, too, in our marriages and when interacting with our kids. But we've learned quite a bit from asking Patty's favorite question: "Why?"

So, let's do it here, together. The timing for this type of exploration is perfect, and you're not alone in turning inward to find peace and understanding. It seems more and more of us are curious about who we are and how to become a better version of ourselves. People in surprising numbers are taking personality tests like Myers-Briggs and the Enneagram, listening to motivational speakers such as Tony Robbins and Oprah Winfrey, and reading self-help books, which include *The 7 Habits of Highly Effective People* and *The Power of Positive Thinking*. There is a movement happening of individual and communal enlightenment and the journey is best begun through questioning what we believe we know, who we believe we are, and how we believe we got here.

Let's start our questions with one about life. Why is life so easy one moment and almost impossible the next? Part of the answer is in that simple example put forth earlier. We assign emotions, feelings, and intentions and predict future outcomes based on circumstances. If you're feeling called out right now, please know we all do it. It is one of many ways humans feel safe. If we went through life and ignored the circumstances, focusing only on goals, we would be robots. Instead, we have rich inner lives that allow us to feel as we live, opening new neural pathways in repeating circumstances that reinforce whether or not something is likely to be positive, fun, safe, unsafe, or boring in the future. This happens without conscious thought. It happens automatically in the subconscious.

If we are lucky and we only have positive circumstances for an entire day, we can enjoy a positive outcome without working for it, easy, simple, and uncomplicated. Many little children believe this about life. It is through growing up, receiving responsibilities, and learning empathy when observing others' hard times that we literally learn to be guarded and careful, assigning intentions and feelings to events. The way each person does this will be different. We will dive into these differences soon.

Let's move on to people. Why is it that we can get along great with one person, but another person drives us crazy? First, it is important to realize that as often as we have this experience with others, of course, they are having it about us! Often, our value system comes into play here, which is all part of our self-understanding. If we were raised to value hard-working people who live simply and do not draw attention to themselves, it makes sense that we can have an automatic reaction to someone who is flaunting the very traits we were conditioned to dislike. Sometimes, we do not dislike the human; we dislike what they represent.

If, however, it is a clash of personalities, this also is its own value system. We decide the qualities we like and respect in others. Remember when Patty said earlier that we (Sal and Patty) both ended up married to people with personality styles that complement ours and people we love just being around? This reflects them possessing the values and traits that we like and think well of. It would be a very different situation if we had each married someone who rubbed us the wrong way. Are there people in your life who rub you the wrong way or who cause you to see red when you are around them?

Often, here, the person is the event, and their value system is the circumstance, and the outcome is either positive or negative, depending on the compatibility of underlying values. A value system can be where they spend their money, how they prioritize education or religion, the topics they discuss, etc. As children and young adults, we are imprinted with ideas of what is good and what is bad. It can help create at least surface-level peace in your social relationships if you can start to see the other person as a neutral event with inherent beliefs, priorities, biases, and triggers that may not line up with yours. And that is okay.

And finally, let's talk about the human brain. Why does every student's hand go up in 2nd grade, but not in 5th? As children, we can be so free. Free of fear of judgment, free of insecurities, and free of inhibitions. Of course, there are always exceptions to this, but in general, kids haven't learned how to build up the walls that come with adulthood. As adults, we have learned that sharing too much can leave us empty, that speaking up can get us ridiculed, and that being kind can lead to betrayal. We learn these lessons through the many events of elementary school, middle and high school, and college.

As a child and teenager, your subconscious mind seeks validation and safety. We want to be validated (have a positive circumstance during an event so that we can enjoy a positive outcome without working for it) to the degree that as we explore, we will return to the things that feel good until, over the years we tend to narrow that explorative circle down into a fairly well-established comfort zone. We learn how far to go until it hurts, so we don't go any farther. We want to be safe because it is our human instinct to stay alive and to feel comfortable. This further encourages us to stay in our comfort zone.

The questions we have posed here are just the most obvious ones. You probably have many more you would like to explore. The layers of "why" can go deeper and deeper. For some, you may feel that your comfort zone is holding you back from asking too many questions. And that is okay. We ask that you start right where you are and take this journey one step at a time. As you read through this chapter, you may have felt something stirring within you, a call to uncover your own personal "why" from within the deepest, most private parts of your mind, heart, and soul.

Let's honor that stirring within. Take a moment and think of a few of those nagging or recurring questions you ask that have held deep in your mind over the course of your life when you think about humanity and why we do the things we do. As we journey through this book, we believe you will build the necessary tools to find answers.

We believe who we are as adults is a combination of all the variables that create one's life. Some variables are delivered to us by choice, while others are without our awareness or consent. Still, each has a timely impact on our evolution. We believe that after the first twenty-one years of life, you have settled into patterns of being, doing, thinking, and feeling. But these patterns can be expanded upon and evolve for your greater good.

Exercise

Take a moment (or several) to breathe deeply. We've covered a lot of material already, with much more to come. Your mind might be whirring rapidly as it absorbs each piece of information. So, pause here and reconnect with your body's energy before continuing.

Here, you will find a self-assessment. There is no right or wrong answer, and the more honest you are, the more you can see your true self and love each part of who you are.

Please answer these questions with your first thoughts (in detail).

1. How do you interact with people?
    - Authoritative___
    - Engaging___
    - Reactive___

2. Are you driven?

3. What is one of your memories around 7 years old?

4. What is one of your memories around 14 years old?

5. What is one of your memories around 21 years old?

6. Who makes you feel uncomfortable?

7. Is control an issue?

8. Do you make the same decisions over and over?

9. Rate yourself, 1 – 10?
   Example: Depends on what. As a human being trying to do my best…9.

10. What challenges have you overcome?

11. What is your biggest challenge?

12. What are you good at?

13. Do you really listen?

14. What makes you cry?
    Example: When someone experiences happiness through persistence.

15. Are you empathetic?

16. Are you sympathetic?

17. How do you define success?
    Example: Accomplishing a goal established by 2 or more.

18. Do you ever worry?

19. Do you think you are smart?

20. Who is your family?

21. Do you have a great life lesson?

22. When is work fun?

23. Are you respected by your peers?

24. Do you follow the rules?

25. Has God ever been present in your life?

26. Are you faithful?

27. Can you run fast?

28. Has someone directly affected your life?

29. Are you competitive?

30. Do you look for the easy way out?

31. What makes you laugh?
    Example: Everyday life being articulated by someone.

32. What hurts your feelings?

33. Describe your first party?

34. Describe trust?

35. What is your definition of love?

36. Who was your first crush?

37. When did you first feel like a grown-up?

38. What was your first lesson in relation to money?
    Example: I was 11 years old when my father would not give me $1.00 for something to eat (sporting event out of town) – a friend's parent bought me a $.59 cent hamburger.

39. What is your favorite time of day?

40. How do you like to study?

Were the questions hard for you; or like most things in life lent themselves to several answers based on the circumstances and time of an event?

Over the next 5 chapters, we are going to take a deeper dive into the most important person in your life, YOU. Why are you the way you are. Who is the person you became? What is your comfort zone? How have you decided to attack life? Have you arrived at peace?

CHAPTER 2

Why – Assigned without Consent

(Ages 0-7)

"Babies are such a nice way to start people." Don Harold

Do you remember the first seven years of your life? Maybe you have a memory or two that you can recall with ease. These immediate memories are usually either full of extreme joy or a degree of pain and are laced with underlying emotions. These event-based memories are easy to recall because, in some way, they influence our lives or our surroundings.

According to research, most people only have memories from around age 3 or 4 onward. This is because the hippocampus, the part of the brain that stores memories, is still developing during the first few years of life. As the hippocampus matures, it becomes better at storing and retrieving memories. However, it is still possible to have memories from earlier in life, especially if they are emotionally charged.

It could be the first wedding we attended of a much older cousin or family member, the loss of a family pet, or the first day in a new school. If we think harder, we can usually recall smaller, less momentous occasions from the first seven years of our lives. These things can be when our parents let us eat ice cream before dinner, or when we made a "best friend" pact with a friend from school. Each moment is meaningful and also carries with it corresponding emotions. Apart from these larger moments imprinted on our brains are the thousands of thoughts, interactions, words, and behaviors that were the total of our day-to-day activities. These often-mundane daily parts of being alive are what created our history. Our *own personal history* and isn't that amazing? *Our* foundation, that is the *least recognizable* time in a human's life, is a significant part of what creates the true us? That's quite a thought!

Memories are stored in the brain in a network of connections between neurons. When we remember something, these connections are activated, and we can experience the memory as if it were happening again. The more often we remember something, the stronger the connections become, and the easier it is to remember.

Let's take young athletes of today. These maturing minds are often coached by parents, mentors, big brothers; people that love and support them and want to see them do their absolute best. For those endless hours on the field, we thank you.

The coach makes decisions, and why does he do that? And how? And what's the impact? Billy, a 12-year-old running back is mid-stride taking the team to the goal line. All-of-a-sudden, there is a moment when the coach (aka Dad) pulls the developing A-player and inserts his son (Johnnie) with the hope of giving him the winning touchdown experience.

The *real* impact and understanding is with the young athletes. Johnnie, Billy, and the whole team saw and felt a decision from the coach's past, which could imprint their present and future.

Memories are a complex and fascinating part of our lives. They help us to make sense of the world and to understand who we are. They also connect us to our past and help us build a sense of identity.

Memories are vital and can be gathered deeply into our minds as either short-term or long-term memories. The sensory receptors in our bodies take in our experiences each day through taste, smell, touch, sight, and sound, but not every memory is easily accessible. And many of our early memories are of events or people we had no control over. Remember how young and dependent we were.

So why do things in our lives that we did not select for ourselves and that we may or may not easily remember have such an impact on us? We believe it to be for three reasons, which are completely out of our control.

We all started with a Birthday

When was that day of birth? Clearly, for the most part, it's unique to each of us. Was it a Sunday evening after sunset? Were we born in January? Or June? Many believe that there are energy sources that are much vaster than we as humans could begin to comprehend. And throughout history, individuals have studied things greater than Earth and man, from God to the Big Bang Theory, from the solar system to Greek mythology, from the miraculous seven wonders of the world to the simplest of things like the air we breathe.

So, let's look at the zodiac (Astrology) and why it impacts human outcomes. There are twelve signs—each assigned to specific dates and times. They represent unconscious feelings, tendencies, and behaviors of a person's life.

We were given a Name

This is the next most influential variable in our "Why" equation. Have you ever stopped to consider your name and its implications? This study of what is in a name will come from various origins, with religion leading the way. And as it is often said… everything can be boiled down to a number. Did you know that? This is an ID badge for life, and we'll talk about what that means for you.

The final piece to the puzzle unveiled in this chapter will look at the uncontrollability of family. We'll look at birth order, family roles, and family expectations. Were you the first, second, or third child, the first boy or second girl? What characteristics and traits do you exhibit that stem from your birth order? We'll also look at the role of family dynamics and the ways nature conflicts with or supports nurturing and how that may have impacted you. Again, these are completely out of our control.

NATURE vs NURTURE

Nature	Nurture
Nature refers to biological heredity and genetic predispositions inherited by individuals from their parents at birth.	Nurture is used to describe environmental factors that influence an individual's development.
This includes physical characteristics such as physical stature, athleticism, and intellect.	This includes a variety of influences, such as parenting style, educational experiences, and cultural background.

Let's move into the first topic, astrology, but before we do, please note that the examples given in this chapter are specific to Patty and serve only as an example of how these different pieces of the puzzle work together for *her*. Your astrology chart, name, and birth order will, of course, produce your unique results. We offer Patty's here to illustrate further how these parts of life contribute to a whole person.

What is in a sign?

Astrology is the utilization of heavenly patterns from celestial bodies to predict humans' personalities, behaviors, and tendencies. Often used in determining an astrological chart is your date, time, place of birth, and other personal information. If you have yet to learn your sign nor have you ever had a birth chart made for you, this can be accomplished through a simple internet search where a plethora of folks can create one for you.

In astrology, the Sun and Moon are considered planets. Each planet represents one or more specific aspects of the person. Let's take a look at the planets in our solar system and the traits they are said to represent.

The Sun: ego structure, personality, etc.

The Moon: feelings, dreams, etc.

Mercury: logic, communication, etc.

Venus: love, romance, etc.

Mars: aggression, forcefulness, etc.

Jupiter: optimism, expansive attitude, etc.

Saturn: responsibility, limitation, etc.

Uranus: unpredictability, higher thought, etc.

Neptune: spirituality, religion, etc.

Pluto: money, sexuality, etc.

What Astrology Can Look Like in Practice

No two individuals are alike, but individuals born on the same date, at the same time, in the same year will have the same astrological chart. The same chart… yes, the same person… no. To give an example of what types of information can be in a chart, Patty offered hers so you can know what to expect when you research your chart. This is simply a matter of using the resources available to each of us, the world wide web. Again, this is just *one* of a few ways we will discuss in this chapter something as seemingly a matter of fact as our birth date that can hold long-term ramifications for our entire adult lives.

Ready?...

So, here's my reaction to my sign… It's SPOT ON!?! And I have to say I was quite relieved to know all of this after years of periodically struggling with how I could've possibly offended that person and why in the world did she react that way? And I could never understand why people didn't like me, although that didn't happen too often. And isn't it always the folks we feel like we're walking on eggshells around that we tend to clash with? I enjoy more than anything small group discussions and one-on-one conversations where I can get to know someone. What knowing myself does for me is help me recognize that everyone has a special story. I learned to recognize that everybody's mojo is not to tell strangers their lifelong secrets. I learn to love others where they are. We all grow up eventually. It takes some of us longer than others. ☺

Looking back, I now admit that my mom and I are total opposites. I could never completely understand "WHY" she didn't gravitate towards me like most others did. My dad was always my biggest fan and liked to discuss things to the point of understanding. Not my mom. Nor many of my bosses. It's business, and it's their business, so "Yes sir" is often the preferred response. Questions and ideas are not typically welcome; I learned that the hard way after truly understanding myself. This gravitational pull I apparently have (and now I know) can be beneficial or detrimental. I *could sense* that at times, yet I wasn't aware *enough* to apply it gracefully, shall we say. Don't abuse your stuff. By plowing through this incredibly insightful workbook… and we have Sal to thank for that, you will learn as I did; there's so much out there to build upon and grow.

Energy came naturally to me based on when I was born. Yes, I like to be alone and in nature and invigorated by people. But not too many at once. All these weird quandaries I'd sometimes ponder. It was intuition, and low and behold, I was correct. So, here's me. Take it as an example of what you may learn about yourself.

Be *ready* when you do. Instinctually, we may fight what you learn initially. It's okay. I did at times, but I got through it. It's natural. We've pictured ourselves one way for so long, and if you're one of those that puts great thought into things like I tend to, only to understand that we've forked down the wrong road, it's not an easy pill to swallow.

LIFE IS EASY

November 1964 (Patty's birth)

The Sun: These highly capable individuals are particularly good at running a business or family...

The Moon: Vivid individuals who are not afraid to flaunt their differences...

Mercury: Quite outspoken, those with Mercury in this position speak their mind straight out...

Venus: Those with Venus here usually have an easy manner with people...

Mars: These people are most effective when they are able to use their energies logically...

Jupiter: A great love of the outdoors and wildlife accompanies this position...

Saturn: Extreme introversion is the greatest danger when Saturn is found here...

Uranus: An interest in all things strange and unusual is characteristic...

Neptune: If isolation and nursing private resentments and grudges manifest here...

Pluto: Cultivating an air of mystery, these folks are not easy to understand, nor do they wish to be understood...

To find how your stars line up, you can use the World Wide Web or other resources found at the local book store. Heck, you might even visit a psychic.

Date of Birth:

1. The Sun:

_____

_____

_____

2. The Moon:

3. Mercury:

4. Venus:

5. Mars:

6. Jupiter:

7. Saturn:

8. Uranus:

9. Neptune:

10. Pluto:

What is in a Name?

The next most identifying variable in the Why equation is the name which we have been given. This can come from a variety of origins, with religion leading the way. We may already remember Sal in the Bible. How about Paul (a Disciple), who was originally named Sal? He was arguably the hardest and most stubborn to change, but the most loyal in the end. Do you know a Paul?

Take a moment and search the internet for the meaning of your name. We will ask that you wait to take your deep dive until after you read Patty's example so that you know more about how to interpret the results you may find online about your name. As we grow and learn our label, we will see that, much like the stars, it has meaning and substance. The power of our name is something bestowed upon us by our parents or families and drives home the point, again, that this is another piece of the puzzle, part of our lives, if you will, where we were not able to influence.

Let's break down the name "Patricia" and its connected numerology, traits, and characteristics, as seen in many people who carry that name.

Patricia

Patricia is a common name for girls. It is of Latin origin and derived from the word patrician, which means "noble." Its male form is Patrick. Some of the short forms of this name are Pat, Pati, Patsy, Trish, etc. Also, we find that Patricia's Expression or Destiny number is said to be five. Based on the idea that numbers hold the key to our innermost personality, as each letter equals a number and each number has a meaning.

Here is what the numerology for me (Patty) says.

The actual number five normally appears quite attractive to the opposite sex. The negative trait of the number five is being too optimistic...

You have more lovers than haters in your life, Patricia. Accordingly, the number five means you enjoy somewhat challenging things...

The particular positive aspect of your expression number is a constantly idealistic attitude...

Most Patricias hold a powerful make-up. You get bored so easily. Occasionally you may act erratic and try to keep everyone pleased...

The actual negative qualities that you hold are associated with stress. You hold an inner feeling of being anxious, and you feel tension; you might be too delicate and also temperamental at work. A person named Patricia will tend to live in a dream world …

As we can see, each name will contain positive and negative traits.

I still remember the first time I saw the meaning of my name. Its accuracy astounded me… I couldn't help but think to myself, *are these people in my head*? Where does this strangely accurate depiction/research come from, and how? Remember, I'm always about the 'why'! Now I want to know 'how'. How in the world does this translate? I mean, "c o m e o n" …like this is freaky insightful! I'm the one gaining the insight. And I love it.

I savored what I learned as it hit home. Getting to the finish line like Dennis the Menace; starting 5 projects at once while four of the five typically resemble nothing close to a straight line. Do I finish what I start? Most of the time, but not always. Living very idealistically and expecting a great deal from people, then plummeting with disappointment when stuff, usually people's stuff, don't fit into place. Or I had to do it by myself.

There is so much more I could share, but for yourself, you go as deep as you want or need to.

It's hunky-dory to know ourselves and be cool with who we are, but we gotta take the next step as we all have relationships with people. We interact with countless people, each with their own story, birth date, name, and history, and we want to navigate those relationships seamlessly with all of our newfound knowledge. All this intel helps, whether standing in line at the grocery store, sitting next to a stranger on the plane, or driving from A to B in crazy traffic. Life at work. Life at home. Life at leisure. Life. Love. And the pursuit of happiness. (I couldn't resist.) See, here we go again…

And your name is? Again, like in the previous section, a chance to discover something more about yourself (the meaning of your name). Use the World Wide Web or other resources found at the local bookstore.

LIFE IS EASY

Name:

Unconscious Identity is the "ID"

We opened the chapter by revealing the impact of the first seven years of life on how we will be as adults. Part of knowing the "Why" is knowing our identity, our ID. This ID is formulated from birth to age seven. Psychoanalytic Theory suggests that the ID is one of three parts of the psyche: the ID, the SuperEgo, and the Ego. The ID is in charge of many of our most primitive functions and will be highlighted here. Many people may associate a name or birth chart as their identity, but another layer is worth looking into.

ID is defined as a division of the psyche and is completely unconscious. It happens outside of our control, organically and naturally. This part of ourselves is where the drives and needs of a person come from, and each of us has a different set of each. These integral parts of ourselves are instinct-driven, and our psychic energy comes from here. We each have basic instincts that tell us when and how much pleasure, satisfaction, and gratification we require to feel alive or happy.

This intuitive part of who we are runs our biological systems, our impulses, and urges and tends to remain stable over the period of our lives. It can feel very infantile in how it functions and manifests itself because it's not impacted by reality, logic, or our environment. It is the part of us that can seem selfish to others or full of wishful thinking or fantasies. It defies logic and rational mental processes. As separate as it is from our intellectual reasoning, it is essential to recognize and embrace it. It is part of our ID and drives many of our most basic decision-making processes and reactions, particularly under stress.

Specifically, the ID is said to control the person's dependence, sexual, and aggression impulses. When one of these impulses gets blocked, humans will lash out, withdraw, freeze, or, in some other way, immediately resolve the issue in an often illogical and emotional way. Additionally, the ID part of the psyche works the same way with or against the other parts of the psyche, namely the Ego and the SuperEgo, which we will discuss in Chapters 3 and 4.

We will now move into birth order, and how you were nurtured (family) may have impacted your adult identity.

As the 5th child, I viewed my older siblings as a road map to all things exciting that would eventually come my way. From being in the car when Patty had her 1st driving lesson in the church parking lot (shaken, not stirred) to toting a victory bell for Mary and the ball team (on the gridiron), observing Paul earn a car through a job (freedom) and then Steve, running wildly through elementary school on Fall Festival Night (crazy train). Everything seemed so simple and easy, but little did I know I was participating in their lives, not mine. Additionally, my father and mother's nurturing support of those first four darling children was not how I would be seen.

I went from being the baby of the family to being a middle child in the blink of an eye. As Patty eloquently wrote (Chapter 1), the first four children were 4 years apart. Then me, 3 years later. My little brother (number 6) was born when I was seven. It was an extremely trying time for our entire family as well. Dad was sick, Mom just had my little brother, Jeff, and I was hit by a car. I was hospitalized for three weeks and spent the next several months in a body cast. The cast did not allow me to sit; therefore, I was transported to school in the back of a station wagon and remained in a reclining lawn chair for the entirety of the school day. It was here that I started to notice the differences in how people interacted with each other and how those differences made me feel (challenging my ID). However, I played backyard football in that cast and survived many gotcha moments from my older brothers, "assholes."

Returning to the shift from the baby of the family to a middle child, this was not really on my radar until Jeff became my responsibility. I was in my world, doing my things, living my life, then all of a sudden as my elder siblings began to graduate… the little guy became my assignment. Now I'm the oldest. The seemingly responsible one. I'll never forget one night, taking him midnight sledding with classmates as "the babysitter," hoping to beat Mom and Dad back home only to find lights on in the house. All I could think about was escaping the situation and dealing with it later… "Get out of the car, Jeff. I'm out of here."

Birth Order Explained

Now that we know how birth order can show up in a sibling or family dynamic, let's look at generally accepted traits of birth order. Hopefully, your family dynamics will come to light more as you learn.

Most **first-born children** will become confident, self-assured, and fairly independent because of attentive parents trying to figure out parenting standards and habits. Why is this? Parents often do their best to fuss over small things, sticking to details until everything is just right. As a result, the child immediately learns that perfectionism matters in life. Being the first child, they also have the luxury of more focused attention placed upon them. Most often but not always, this will foster a strong sense of personal value in the child and a belief that they matter in this world.

First-born kids tend to manifest leadership traits early on and be forced to shoulder many additional responsibilities if additional siblings enter the family dynamic. This sense of responsibility is generally carried well by them as they learn from their parents that not only do they matter (and therefore their efforts matter), but they are also capable of extra responsibility. As adults carry these beliefs into the world, they may start to burn out if they don't learn how to say "no" to helping others or running the show. People who are firstborn children need to learn to prioritize rest and to prioritize themselves. Taking a break and doing things that might feel frivolous is okay.

> Positive traits usually seen in firstborn kids:
> - Creating structure
> - Manifesting behaviors that are in the "high achieving" category professionally, at school and home (sometimes may feel controlling to others)
> - Being appropriately cautious due to an understanding of the responsibilities involved in each endeavor

Second-born children come into the world often with parents who feel like they have the parenting protocols under control. They see that their first-born child is doing well and feel they don't have the time or attention to devote to their second child as they did to their first child. As a result, many second-born children can feel dismissed and left wondering what is wrong with them. This is not always the case, though. Suppose the second-born child is of a different gender than the first-born child. In that case, they will likely still feel a sense of "I am special, and I matter" because their parents need to be watchful and attentive due to raising a child of a different gender and with different needs.

Very pronounced traits tend to manifest if the second-born child becomes the middle child. With the birth of a third child, the middle child feels a loss of identity. They see the responsible older child helping and being mature while watching the new addition to the family being too helpless to care for themselves. Both strategies (being helpful or being helpless) earn attention from the parents, and often, the middle child resorts to people-pleasing tactics to try to receive the attention they want. They may swing between copying the mature elder child to resorting to tantrums akin to the new baby. Under it all, their cry is for individual attention from the parents.

Some of the positive traits second-born children exhibit:
- Showing up in others' lives as pleasers
- Exhibiting some spurts of rebellion
- Helping during the conflict through peacemaking

The baby of the family or **last-born child** tends to benefit from the experience of their parents. They don't often feel smothered by rules like the first-born child was, and they do not feel forgotten or lacking identity like the middle child (or children) did. Instead, they often will feel freedom. They tend to be agreeable and easy-going people who bring positive energy to social interactions.

Last-born children are used to getting things their way and often have the distractions of their elder siblings to keep the sterner eye of their parents off them. As a result, they may grow up to expect life to go their way and can be experts at working a situation in their favor. After all, they have their older siblings and siblings' friends to observe as teenagers or older kids interact with their parents. Given that there are older siblings, it is reasonable that many last-born kids tend to think the exact opposite of their first-born siblings. Whereas the firstborn believes that every detail is important, the baby of the family tends to relax and think that very few things are important, maybe even that their own choices and behaviors are not important.

Some of the positive traits of the last-born child:
- Preferring to keep things simple and not complicated.
- Knowing how to convince people to give them what they want.
- Feeling a right to take what they need from life without shame.

If you are an **only child**, you will likely identify most with traits of the first-born child. Most children report that their parents showed them vast amounts of attention, expected a lot from them, and supported them. As a result, most children show up in adulthood as leaders who are mature beyond their years and full of self-confidence.

You cannot control when you were born, your name, or the order in which you were born. As you can see, the labels decided for you will have a tremendous impact on your life from birth up to age seven. When you are deeply receiving the spoken and unspoken messages from around you about who you are and how you fit into the bigger picture of your family structure as well as the world. We hope that by seeing these parts of your life more clearly, you can start or continue to unravel the deeper parts of why you act and react in ways you might love or want to improve upon.

Were you first born? Are you the middle child or the last-born? Are you an only child? Do you identify with traits from each category? And remember, your parents were once children too.

Now, take a moment and reflect on your astrological sign, name, and birth order. Can you see that person in the mirror? Use this space to express how you feel about your three different labels.

_____

_____

_____

_____

_____

_____

_____

_____

LIFE IS EASY

CHAPTER 3

Who – Established through Identity

(Ages 7-14)

"Every child has an untold story that needs to be heard." Meetzz

It's time to take a closer look at who we are as we interact with others and figure out our identity about those around us. As our eyes are opened, we realize our value through how others treat us: parents to teachers, siblings to peers, girls and boys, coaches, and persons of authority. Our identity is both reinforced and challenged by those around us constantly and most acutely between the ages of seven and fourteen. These years are crucial for us as our nature is swayed and molded through nurture.

It's as vivid as if it happened yesterday. My very athletic (and competitive) younger sister screams, "It's a race," while I am *pacing* myself at a swim meet in the outside lane, doing the backstroke ricocheting from one side to the other. Hearing the coach's instructions to pace myself, I was doing as I was told. And here we are, almost 50 years later, and the whole bunch of us, including myself, still think of me as the weak link when choosing teams. If it is not a serious competition… the captain will *take me* because of my optimism!

Remember, we just learned that one of Patty's negative name traits was that she might be too optimistic.

Over these seven years (ages seven to fourteen), our social interactions pit unconscious feelings established (0-7) against the reality of situations. At that age, it's reasonable that we do not truly understand who we are and why we are the way we are. Our nature (natural tendencies) may differ greatly from a caregiver (parent or grandparent). We might feel a lot of shame for handling situations because of the feedback or criticism we receive. Conversely, we may feel empowered if our natural tendencies complement theirs and we receive praise. Our feedback loops with parents, authority figures, siblings, friends, and others vastly impacting how we feel about ourselves. A lot of emotional damage can be done during this time that we will then spend a near lifetime leveraging or unpacking, if we are brave enough to dig deep as adults.

Understanding the Ego

Let's look at the human Ego and its role during the pivotal developmental years between ages seven and fourteen. Ego can be defined generally as the self (me) as it is contrasted by another's self (you). Once the Ego has developed, it is responsible for mediating between the unrealistic ID and the reality of life, the situation, or the person's actions. Our Ego uses its interpretation of reality to satisfy its demands and to obtain what it seeks. Much like the ID, the Ego seeks out pleasure by reducing tension that has been created, and avoids pain. It challenges like the ID, but is weak in comparison.

What does all of this mean? Think of a time in your childhood when you distinctly remember an occurrence. You can remember the where, when, who, and… how, and why. Maybe it is a family holiday like Christmas or a big day in your life, like your first day in 5th grade at school. If this big event has come up in conversation with your siblings or parents as you walk down memory lane, the odds are that you all can agree on where the event took place, when it happened, and even who was there. But you may not agree on how events played out. You *may not* agree on why certain things happened or were said.

Each of you may staunchly stand by your recollection of how Aunt Myra handled your cousin showing up late, for example, or why your cousin did not. This happens not because everyone has a faulty memory. It happens because the Ego interprets events in your mind and logs the interpretation away according to your own Ego's bias, not according to rational facts. As you observed and experienced these big events, your brain was cataloging the how and why according to your Ego, and those around you were doing the same.

This is important for many reasons. In the context of this chapter, the importance lies in recognizing that we do have biases and tendencies towards or against interpretations. They are formed when we are young, and shape how we look at life, who we get along with easily, and how we handle conflict when we disagree with others.

When our nature is challenged from age seven to fourteen, we will handle it differently than our siblings. We may shut down emotionally and comply, giving in to the authority figure's feedback loop. Or we may stand up straighter and demand to know why they said what they said. We may turn to complaining, passive aggressiveness, or any reactionary behaviors. As adults, we learn to regulate these natural reactions, but they are still there and they color everything we do. Our Ego (established between ages 7-14) is built around how we feel and how others seem to treat us.

Going back to the example of Aunt Myra and the cousin, each member of your family who recalls the scenario is doing so from their Ego. You may hear your mom form an opinion like, "Your cousin Jackie is always late. It's not a big deal." In this instance, her Ego seeks to dismiss the behavior and possibly protect Jackie. Your sister may say, "Yeah, Jackie was probably hungover from partying the night before. What a mess." And in this instance, her Ego is puffing herself up because she showed up on time and she is putting Jackie down by assuming hers. You might even say, "She wasn't late at all. We were all just early. Stop picking on her." And, finally, your brother may say, "Jackie didn't even drive that day. I bet she was waiting for an Uber."

All of these are opinions of the situation and assumptions of why or how it happened. When we form an opinion and verbalize it, we reveal our biases and the games our Ego can play in our minds. If we have built self-awareness, we can easily see our Ego on display when we start to make verbal assumptions or explain why something happened. Again, this formation of the Ego is most aggressively formed during our younger years. It shows up in every area of our lives, trying hard to protect us and our often-fragile sense of self.

Since our Ego serves as the middleman between our sense of self and the expectations or pressures of the outside world, as adults, we can learn to mitigate our ego-fueled reactions and choose instead to honor that honest inner part of who we are, our ID. For example, when we feel annoyed by our father's repeated negative worldview and want to lash out verbally as an immediate reaction, accusing him of always being sour or mean, we can choose instead to go a layer deeper and ask ourselves, what part of our nature is their negativity threatening? Deep down, his words are in direct violation of some truth, our nature holds dear.

If he was, instead, making excuses for everybody instead of cutting them down, we might have no reaction to that at all because our nature may not have a defensive reaction to that worldview.

If his words trigger us, instead of lashing out, we can be vulnerable and say, "When you cut down my attempts to solve a problem, it makes me feel worthless and inadequate." Or "When you interrupt me with all the ways something won't work out, it makes me feel like you do not value my opinions." Then, he has the option to listen and adjust or choose to cause you pain intentionally. If we do not let others close to us know how they make us feel, they are not responsible for the outcome. If we lash out in our Ego and hide the hurt underneath, they may see us as a challenging person and double down in their stance. Being vulnerable and honest with our true selves gives others a chance to make an adjustment in themselves, which, ultimately, will strengthen our bond with them. This is especially important within family dynamics.

Our Ego may want to lash out to protect ourselves or to make us feel big and strong, but, ultimately, this is destructive for the relationship. It is fascinating to realize that all the foundation of the Ego is being formed at such a young age! Age seven to fourteen is the time when our unconscious is being challenged. Every occurrence or situation creates a new feeling that gets added to who we see ourselves as being and allows us to learn our unique communication styles and our temperament. When a new situation arises, we subconsciously ask ourselves, is it easy, does it feel good, do we hide, or are we uncomfortable in our skin?

In school, no matter how good one is, 12-year-old girls can find a way to build conflict. So, there are 8 of us between 2 sixth grade classes and the school decided to try a little intervention. During numerous lunch hours, our little clique is taken to a place where we can speak freely. I remember each of us being asked to divide $1.00 among the group according to who we trusted, and I will never forget receiving .85 cents from Sherry. At the time, it struck me more than I realized. Today, I can hardly tolerate a friend I cannot trust.

Our natural state is being reinforced or condemned, building a life perspective. We usually find ourselves gravitating to like-minded people or people in proximity to our temperament. We want to feel good, to be free of pain or conflict as children, so the Ego is the main way we manage our social and familial interactions.

Before we move on to how our Ego fits into our self-esteem, let's pause and affirm that having an Ego is a human experience. Our Ego will always be there. We are not criminalizing the Ego or claiming it does not help us. What we do believe is that being aware of our Ego and learning to manage it is important to have a fulfilled life. When we do not allow our Ego to control our reactions and reactionary words, we can walk more freely and form deeper bonds with those close to us. The Ego wants us to feel good, but it often does that in ways that break down bonds of connection or cause harm to self and others. Learning to see when we are acting in Ego versus acting from our natural self will empower and liberate us.

Self–Esteem - Fostering Confidence and Satisfaction in Oneself

Self-esteem is the way we value ourselves and how we perceive ourselves. Unlike our Ego which can be formed and remain firmly in place, our self-esteem can change from day to day or experience to experience. We may feel strong and in control in some situations and our self-esteem is at peace because we do not feel fear of failure. Still, in the very next situation or if a new variable is introduced then all of a sudden, our self-esteem is lowered several notches. We may go from being gregarious and joyful, to quiet and shy. We may go from patient and understanding to judgmental or impatient. Being aware of these changes will help us to recognize our patterns and decide if we want to keep them or improve them.

Our self-esteem is developed during the same range, ages seven to fourteen, as the Ego but the evolution continues as we mature through life. Our nature is constant, but the variable of nurture sends messages about who we are and who we should be. Let's talk about this in three scenarios: peers, authority figures, and society.

The judgment of our peers is felt acutely during those formative years. Remember when we talked about the hand going up in 2nd grade but not 5th grade? Our friends, classmates at school, strangers within our age range, or our siblings and their friends all create their feedback loops with us. *We are **all** doing it!* This lets us know through words and reactions, or even facial expressions, all the ways our nature is not good enough. If we have a sibling who excels at sports, naturally fast and agile, and who receives copious amounts of praise from our parents for their athleticism, we may feel small or lacking when our nature prefers the sweet sounds of classical music or the violin in lieu of the hard-hitting tendencies of sports. We may be allowed or verbally encouraged to take violin lessons. Still, the feedback loop we observe between our parents and our athletic siblings can leave lasting impressions of us not being good enough. This can damage our self-esteem as it also shapes us to believe that one hobby is better or has more value than another. We may continue our hobby but downplay our talent or never fully realize it because the subconscious messages we received were that our hobby or talent was not as important. This can happen with any of the messages we receive about or from our siblings or peers.

How our authority figures (parents, teachers, religion, the law, etc.) interact with us also can shape our view of ourselves. If we see our parents tense up every time a police officer comes by, the subconscious message we as children receive is, "Cops are to be feared. They can hurt us." Our self-esteem in this instance shrinks around law enforcement or other governmental factions. If our teachers praise only the final grade and not the effort, again the message we receive can be that no matter how hard we try, we'll never measure up.

The impact that society (or our perceived value through media, social media, etc.) has on us cannot be overstated. Each day, we are shown what the ideal human should be through politicians, celebrities, and influencers. If we do not match up to what society says is good or desirable, the feedback loop to us is that we are less than others. When faced with this reality, people may use their Ego to try to completely alter their personality to fit what is being praised or go so far as to alter their physical appearance permanently. The root cause is that our self-esteem so desperately wants to be validated and recognized as being good enough that we chase the latest fad, hoping to feel secure and loved.

And that is ultimately what our nature wants: love. The Ego is constructed to help us avoid pain and to feel good, and the tactics our Ego uses can be a substitute for receiving love. We let our Ego say cutting words to feel powerful to hide how small we feel inside. Or we let our Ego hold people at arm's length when deep down we yearn for closeness. And woven through all of this is our often-wounded self-esteem that is trying to work through the barrage of messages telling us all the ways we are not quite enough.

As you can see, this normal human experience (between the ages of 7-14) might be of some importance to start to untangle and work through as an adult. At this point, you may feel a tad overwhelmed, especially if this is your first-time diving into these concepts. Rest assured, this is normal, and each of us uses these tactics until we walk the narrow path toward self-love, love of others, and gradual dissection and rearrangement of our Ego and self-esteem. It's not always easy, but you can make it through to the other side.

"Life is in front of you, not behind." rjn

Through a renewed perspective, convey 3 to 5 memories from ages 7 – 14 regarding family, school, friends, sports, activities, opposite sex, etc.

Example: Friday night lights, and I was goo-goo over a girl. Although my feelings were strong, I was easily derailed by a group of older female students. Ones I knew, but not well enough to be aware of their animosity toward my newfound crush. I never saw it coming. I was befriended by the pack and brought into a circle I had no business being a part of (my go-along to get along nature). Convinced to be a pawn in someone else's game. Not once, but twice (Sorry ☹). What a fool I was. A decision that placated so much of my teenage years and beyond that I sometimes wonder, What if?

_____

_____

_____

_____

LIFE IS EASY

CHAPTER 4

What – Reinforced by Approval

(Ages 14 – 21)

"Actions speak louder than words."

PSA: We hope Chapters 2 and 3 were enlightening and you're still with us after learning about your ID and Ego. For this Chapter, it is said to be even a little more text-booky, unlike the ages of 14-21. When each of us was coloring outside the lines, beating to our own drum in a partly cloudy state of mind.

As we grow up, we start to become aware of the effect of our choices, as well as see what happens when others make choices and take action toward *their* desires and goals. By the time we reach the age of 14, we have observed and experienced enough of life to know what is okay and what is not in most circumstances. We consider the next seven years incredibly important and to be transformative. From ages 14 to 21, we tailor ourselves toward the approval of others, allowing the "what" of ourselves to be reinforced by that same approval.

It is during this time that the SuperEgo steps front and center, and solidifies the moral compass and character that will guide us for the rest of our lives. Our comprehension of what is right or wrong and why becomes deeply held during the ages of 14 to 21. The SuperEgo is neither good nor bad, but it does hold huge sway over the inner voice that lives in our minds until the day that we die. Let's look at what the SuperEgo is and how it nails down what we are.

I think back to those years and clearly see myself as an attentive student, sitting in the front of the class, involved in extracurricular activities, making friends with everybody I met, and remembering how people trusted me most. And throughout life, that is exactly what I expected. A two-way street filled with mutual trust and respect. I trust and respect you; you trust and respect me. When that lollipops and roses (Ego) perspective was challenged one too many times, I finally had to figure something else out. Recognizing, everyone has their own story. Everyone is not an open book. Everyone has their own "what."

The first part of the SuperEgo is often called our conscience, the inner judge and jury we carry with us that tells us certain behaviors, words, and reactions are bad or will bring us consequences. Our conscience is our guide for fitting into the family expectations we have grown up with, the societal expectations we have learned, and the expectations from our peers and authority figures. It would be inappropriate, for example, to say certain things around your grandparents that we might say to our brother or sister or to a friend. If we accidentally spoke too freely around a respected elder, we could feel an immediate wave of guilt. We may blush or feel embarrassed. This reaction is our SuperEgo sending clear signals that you have violated a familial expectation or norm. No one has to say anything to us or reprimand us. The SuperEgo does that automatically, and if left unchecked can make us feel much worse about a situation than we need to, before we make things right. Just because our conscience is yelling at us in our mind does not mean we must automatically believe the severity of those thoughts.

Dad says, "Are you really going out in public looking like that?" Thinking that skirt is way too short.

Daughter says, "Well, yea... everybody's wearing it." Thinking Dad is so out of touch. I'd rather be accepted by my friends than please my Dad.

Dad says, "So if everyone jumped off a bridge, you'd jump too?" Thinking, holy cow, I know how my parents felt, but is this a battle to wage?

We need the conscience to help navigate through the often-complex social rules, but we also need to be aware of the critical inner voices we have. There might be some instant criticisms that arise from the SuperEgo that we need to let go of. We may need to remind ourselves that we are only human and cannot be perfect or hold ourselves to such a high standard that we feel crushed when things do not go perfectly. If we start to allow our SuperEgo to dictate our conscience instead of shaping it, we could begin to self-punish or create consequences for ourselves to cement a lifelong lesson. This part of the SuperEgo is too extreme to be healthy and should be kept in check.

It was a new season, with a continued desire to play ball, and I restricted my participation. Not playing the previous year, I had convinced myself it was not right to regain status as a ballplayer nor fair to my classmates to compete for positions they had earned.

Sal was a teenager, and I'm in my 50's, yet I still experience this. I consistently hold myself back when dealing with industry professionals. Feeling that I am less than. Never feeling like I have earned or can earn their respect because of my perspective that I am less than them. Knowing this not to be true, I still allow this to hold me back from the fruits of my labor.

Both scenarios illustrate a sense of fear, a fear of experiencing pain from our self-esteem while submitting to our ID.

The second part of the SuperEgo is the ego ideal. This is how we see ourselves as human beings living among other humans. We want to aspire to the ideals espoused in our family unit, our schools, what we see on social media, and in our friend groups. We know in the core of our being what is considered ideal or desirable by those crucial parts of our lives and the ego ideal spurs us on to achieving as much of that image as we can.

In layman's terms, the SuperEgo is how you want to be seen.

It is amazing to consider that the development of the SuperEgo starts at age fourteen. This is a time when we are starting to become more aware of the world around us as well as the expectations others have of us. We are also starting to develop our sense of morality and ethics. The conscience is a part of the SuperEgo that tells us "no" when we are about to do something wrong. It helps us to avoid making choices that could harm ourselves or others. The ego ideal is another SuperEgo part that motivates us to do good or obtain our wants. It helps us to strive for excellence and to be the best people we can be.

When the conscience and the ego ideal are balanced, we can make good choices that align with our values. We are also able to feel good about ourselves and our accomplishments. However, if the conscience or the ego ideal is too strong, it can lead to problems. For example, if the conscience is too strong, we may become overly inhibited and afraid to take risks. If the ego ideal is too strong, we may become perfectionists and never feel good enough.

Finding a balance between the conscience and the ego ideal is an important part of growing up! Simply put, this allows us to feel good about ourselves and live a happy and fulfilling life. Here are some ideas for developing a healthy SuperEgo.

- Understand your ego and how it was developed. *Fun to explore.*
- Challenge your feelings with open and vulnerable communication. *The importance of a mentor.*
- Try not to concede to making others' lives easier while you respect their position. *A true grind.*

When we are young children, our ID has a plethora of urges that may not be ideal, but as we grow up, we learn to repress, suppress, and/or execute on these urges. We start to label them and push them away on our path toward maturity. Some of this suppression is good. We don't, after all, want to hit someone for stealing our favorite toy. But other impulses we repress can be less good if it leads to us isolating or holding people at arm's length from fear of rejection or failure.

This would be a great time to pause and reflect on some of the innocent urges we may want to act on or minimize. We all have them… relax, reflect, and release to feel more like yourself.

What do we do, don't do or say, today, that creates harm to ourselves and others?

_____

_____

_____

_____

The SuperEgo is a layered part of what we are, and it is worth asking ourselves a question as we start to unpack how the SuperEgo may be shaping our life. *Are we becoming what we want to be or morphing into something different?* It is completely healthy and okay to challenge the SuperEgo and make sure the voices in our minds are not too harsh, even if we fall short of an expectation placed upon us. Or placed by us.

As these expectations are becoming foundational to us, we as teenagers will have little to no idea that it is taking place. We will merely know that some of our behaviors make us feel bad and others make us feel good. We will notice that when our siblings or friends do things, they are either rewarded or punished. Our subconscious mind begins to build a complex and layered framework of what is good versus what is bad. If left unchallenged in our adulthood, we could still be living with the pressures and standards built by a very young teenage mind.

Do you still hear the voices of your mother or father in your head?

This is the period in our life where what we become is solidified. We are learning by reinforcement, approval, acceptance, and determination. We develop qualities that will carry us through our relationships and our career. Grit, mental resolve, commitment, determination, and hard work become established during this time as our ego ideal assesses what is praised and strives to push us toward that positive sense of self. We learn that what we put in is what we get out.

During this time (ages 14-21), we might recall feeling that our self-esteem was through the roof, and many things felt so close to our reach. At the same time, it is realistic that our self-confidence was questioned by both our inner voice and those around us at every turn. The teenage years are not easy, and the development of the SuperEgo contributes to this.

Like self-esteem, self-confidence is specific to situations and circumstances. When our ID, self-esteem (Ego) and self-confidence partner together the SuperEgo becomes our point of view. This furthers our Communication Temperament. More on this in a moment.

We also learn during this time the power of influence. After all, we are being influenced by those around us, and, naturally, we would want to influence others in ways we are just learning and understanding. Let's take a look at a few. In today's world, amplified by social media coupled with where we grow up, a common separator between young people ages 14 to 21 is finance. When money enters the equation, it becomes a measuring stick for influence and confidence. What we own, what we can go buy, and what family name we carry (social status) all build up our sense of self and further, develop the inner voice we will carry with us for the rest of our lives.

This is when our circumstances (usually uncontrollable) have the most profound impact on life, physically, mentally, and socially. We do not ask what family to be born into or what our social and financial circumstances will be. But we are left navigating through their impact our entire lives. We learn that part of what we are in the eyes of others depends on how we look at them. Does society deem us attractive, fit, and desirable? If so, our self-confidence may soar in this area, and our SuperEgo may push us toward being even better-looking or stronger through self-care rituals. Do our teachers and parents give us feedback that is constructive (positive) or dismissive (negative)? This can impact us mentally, especially if the feedback somehow attacks our identity. A final circumstance that contributes to what we are is the social aspect of our lives. Is our perception of where we fit into society a true reality or just our perception of it?

The biggest impact during this time is if Mom and Dad were present and took an interest in us by choice! Attentive parents tend to send incredibly powerful unspoken messages to their kids that shape their SuperEgo, confidence, and perception of peers and societal structures.

It is at this time in life when a boy turns into a man (needs to able to beat his chest, as the old saying goes, like Tarzan) and when a girl starts to turn into a woman (begins the need for security in everything). Teenagers learn how to make their families react to them and their wants, often using extreme behaviors or words as they try to figure out how to navigate their perceptions of what they are and how they fit into the many structures in their lives. This is a challenging time when confidence builds in one area of life while others can fall short.

Depending on our SuperEgo, we as teenagers may try on many different looks and attitudes to see what is rewarded. This happens as we see what happens around us when we act one way versus another. Once our self-confidence (confidence in oneself and in one's powers and abilities) is rewarded through feedback from others in the parts of our lives we feel are under our control, we start to settle down. Self-confidence is specific to situations and circumstances. And most of our circumstances during that time are out of our control. We are left building ourselves into what we want to become through trial and error that is largely based on the feedback (words, judgments, actions, and reactions) of our peers, family, authority, and society.

I was class president in my Sophomore and Junior years of high school, so wouldn't it make sense that our leadership trio would win the election our Senior Year? 300-plus students did not see it that way, and we lost. To the class partiers of all people! They were our friends... we all were, back in the day. We conceded and followed their lead, their crazy ideas that were not ours, like good sports. Commencement day that Spring was a piece of cake, and we were proud of the guys at the podium. Is this where I learned winning isn't everything? Or that concession is easier?

Once we do enough in certain areas of our lives to feel good and be satisfied, those areas are full of self-confidence. We often learn that it is not who we are but what we do that makes a difference. In all that we accomplish, sometimes **adults or peers** will present us with a false positive form of feedback, thinking it will help us to feel motivated to continue on. Or they may present us with a false negative form of feedback, believing it will keep us on the straight and narrow path. A false positive in this context is making a person believe they achieved a certain result when they did not (often seen in praise that is unwarranted). A false negative is hyping up a failure or pretending that a potential consequence has already occurred. Both forms of feedback are commonly used but are not effective due to their deception. They do, however, impact our self-confidence. If we believe we were given false positives or negatives in our young adult years, now is a great time to reassess how that feedback impacts our inner voice and self-perception.

Ever heard stories that everyone gets a ribbon for participation? If you came in first place or last, you are a winner because you tried. Oh boy! Who came up with this idea? The trophy shop. A practice mostly implemented between the ages of 7-14 (the self-esteem years), then the real world hits back. The real question… has a strength now become a weakness? *Should everyone get a chance to retake every test until they get the grade they want?*

Earlier in this chapter we introduced the concept of our Communication Temperament. This is our disposition that is embedded into our personality. It tends to be validated by self-confidence as we gauge the impact of our words and communication styles. We may learn through feedback from others that our default type of communication works really well for us. As an example, when we communicate in a calm and peaceful way, people stop yelling at us or people come to us with their problems and allow us to help. If our ego ideal likes this, then we will continue developing this temperament. We may discover that our default communication style of being assertive and fearlessly raising our vocal volume calms down volatile situations. If this helps us feel safe, we will continue to build on this natural part of our Communication Temperament.

Depending on our circumstances, we may have seen both extremes modeled for us. We may lean more towards one versus another but will adapt to try to fit into the type of person we want to be perceived as. It is worth noting our own defaults in how we communicate and making sure we are communicating in ways that are authentic to us.

We may also notice that our parents and peers are mostly abstract communicators, talking from their "Why", their "Who", and their "What" – their first twenty-one years of life, rather than listening. See me for who *I* am! We may be more concrete thinkers but will adapt to fit into the communication style that we are exposed to and want to be praised for. If given the opportunity as an adult, we may revert back to our default Communication Temperament if we are in a safe environment and have worked on untangling parts of our SuperEgo.

Refer to the ages of 14 - 21. Keep in mind that you may have experienced significant changes during this period. **LET'S PLAY**…

LIFE IS EASY

1. List 3 accomplishments or examples of recognition received.
   _____
   _____
   _____
   _____

2. How did you interact with your parents?
   Example: Tried to make life as easy as possible for them.
   _____
   _____
   _____
   _____

3. How did you interact with your peers?
   _____
   _____
   _____
   _____

4. How did you interact with your siblings?
   _____
   _____
   _____
   _____

5. Who were your strongest relationships with?

_____

_____

_____

_____

6. What kind of feedback did you receive from coaches, teachers, and/or authority?
   Example: She is such a pleasure to have in class.

_____

_____

_____

_____

CHAPTER 5

How – Means to an End

"Life begins at the end of your comfort zone." Unknown

For the next several years, we believe humans are preoccupied with how things will be accomplished. This period of life is all about the momentum of choice. That means that we are focused on the future and how to arrive at the goals or the idea of happiness we have built for ourselves. This can be a time of confusion or perceived clarity, but truly depends on one's ***expectations*** going forward. An expectation is the idea of what "should" happen or how things "should" be based on our actions today. For example, we should receive an A on a test because of our time studying today. Or we should end up marrying our college sweetheart because of the amount of compatibility we have today and the shared vision for the future that we have today. These 'should' statements are our expectations, but life does not always give us what we expect, and A plus B does not always bring us to C.

This portion of our lives is full of learning the softer skills, whereas, in previous times, our lives were focused on survival skills such as speaking or problem-solving. From age twenty-one on, we are heavily focused on our communication. We have learned that *how* we communicate either brings us what we want or takes what we want further away from us. Our unique way of communicating to meet our needs, collaborate, manipulate, and deliver information to others is called our Communication Temperament. This will be a deliverable for the rest of our lives and will be further solidified as we dig into the tactics that bring about the results we want from others.

This Communication Temperament we each have is built on how we receive information, either from an objective source (a textbook or scientific data) or from a subjective source with their own Communication Temperament at play (a fellow human). Their perception of a situation can influence how they communicate about it and then, in turn influence how they receive the information, process it, and then spread it to others in their own communication style. This is why rumors are so easily built and spread. Each of us may unintentionally focus on a different part of the same story and communicate it in a skewed way.

There are three main parts of our Communication Temperament (**21T**): the Why, the Who, and the What. The "why" (0-7) of our communication is usually subconscious and not something we dig too deeply into. Why are we saying, doing, or coming across in a certain way will usually remain subconscious for us. We are aware of and conscious of the "who" (7-14) of our communication. The "what" (14-21) is a blend of "why" and "who" and is usually only partly conscious. When these three pieces come together in our communication, we deliver words to others based on our interpretations of the circumstances. It makes communication far more nuanced and complex than we may have thought!

We can easily see why young adults often feel misunderstood by their siblings, friends, parents, or co-workers. With their Communication Temperament firmly in place, they may feel like others do not hear them or adequately understand them. Especially in today's world as the widely accepted use of technology blocks non-verbal expression and tone of voice, easily discarding emotional play and adding to our lack of vulnerability. We become fixed in our Communication Temperament by 21 and carry it with us for life.

During this time, we enter the final stages of our maturation process with each person's Communication Temperament completed. Since the brain is fully developed at age 25, we have all of our cognitive prowess to help us navigate life's complex hurdles, caution us when needed, and fuel us with anxiety or questions we may have never faced before. We start to see and understand power dynamics and how people can work a system to get what they want out of it. We set up internal boundaries and fabricate our sense of order and structure. Humans do this to try to remain objective. Boundaries are a way to keep to our rules and our guidelines.

When we are stressed or tired, we can view things more subjectively, which can be a problem with goal setting.

We then become aware of societal boundaries and how people follow the rules or social norms. We are keenly aware of what happens if we do not follow these norms. And internally, our why (ID) and who (Ego), and what (SuperEgo) may be challenged. Many people during this time have a huge struggle with interpreting the experiences happening around them. They know that society keeps moving for the benefit of those in power, and the self agrees with or moves boundaries to lessen the pain. We know how others fit into the societal structures around us, and we maneuver our way into and through them, too.

During this time, achievement is so much predicated on the people or circumstances around us. We know enough to want to achieve goals or lofty accomplishments, but we are not polished enough to muscle through it without being overly impacted by those around us, their ID, Ego, and SuperEgo.

No matter the time in our lives, our teens, 20s, 40s, or even at 60, there's nothing like a mentor. Whenever we start something new, there's simply a sense of peace in knowing we can gently launch into a new world with help. Yes, some of us can jump in without hesitation, but needing a mentor and enjoying a mentorship is fluid. And of course, we'll navigate on our own eventually, but nothing beats that warranted insight all of us should be so fortunate to experience.

A mentor is priceless, be it a new job, a new class, or joining a club for the first time. Mentors matter and solidify the investment. On both sides. And for multiple reasons/resources. If we haven't found a mentor yet, no matter our age… we need to find one. It's never too late. Let us add that the key to this mentorship working is the fit. The compatibility of each person's **21T**.

A productive mentoring relationship raises two people to a place of growth. The effective mentor shares with his potentially new success story the tricks of the trade, the backdoors, and the keys to success that often need to be written in a handbook.

As we can imagine, with both an awareness of what is going on around us and coupled with the assigned boundaries and Communication Temperament, we are caught in a state of flux regarding how we feel about all of this. Do we accept it point blank, or do we deny the ways we are interpreting life? Do we start to look back at our entire lives up to that point and question the things we once took for granted as fact or as unchangeable?

Our parents may have modeled frugality for us, which made us believe that was the only way to be. But now we see others taking big risks with their finances and earning bigger returns. Or we may have been modeled on behaviors that make us feel we must get married by the age of 30 and have two kids. We once took it as a fact that was a non-option, but now we see others succeeding in life as single people. The examples go on and on. This period of questioning our interpretations of life is neither good nor bad. It simply is. And it is a powerful time for young adults. The messages we were sent as kids through parents, teachers, and authority figures are now being seen through the lens of a maturing adult who wants the ability and freedom to do things their way.

This is when a man or woman wants to make all their decisions autonomously. They may push away from authority figures who feel they are trying to impose a way of living onto them. By pushing them away the young adult thinks they will have freedom. This may be a step toward physical freedom, but the ultimate freedom is also a great challenge in one's life – not to become an unknown servant of your past. It is okay to question the past and determine the type of adult you want to be. This is common and healthy.

It also makes sense that this is why musicians say this is their greatest period of creativity. During their twenties, they can fully and freely challenge boundaries per their **21T** and figure out what personal and societal boundaries they want and believe in. People are often more expressive during this time and feel the freest to vocalize their thoughts.

Let's take a moment to talk about *"how"* we come across to others and *"how"* we view the ways we want to come across to others.

How we come across or are perceived by others can be called our presentation, or how we present ourselves to those around us. This usually will begin in our minds. We try on in earlier years the beliefs and attitudes of others and decide what suits us. Once we are in our early twenties, we know what traits we feel good showing to the world. Our Communication Temperament (**21T**) is set. Still, we can show only parts of it to our outer circle, more of it to our middle circle, but rarely all of it to our innermost circle of family and trusted friends.

Our presentation is a personal projection of **21T**, and it is done strategically based on how we truly want others to see us. This is our curated self. We may want to be seen as smart. So, we show that side of our personalities to get a result, maybe a promotion or a reputation for being able to answer tough questions without being anxious. Or we want to be seen as witty, so we show the funny side to our colleagues or acquaintances and the next thing we know we are the one who is called upon in a group to crack a joke or lighten the mood. Once we have presented ourselves to society, we will be given a role and expected to perform. None of this is discussed or fully conscious to people, but it happened on a subconscious level years ago. It can make personal growth hard when we outgrow a role and want to expand into a different one. We may have felt this discomfort a few times over the decades, starting in your mid-twenties. Our social presentation and the roles we fit into can start to feel too small for us on the path toward maturity.

If you're like me, I need an analogy here. There's so much to get through... but that's the hard work. Let's you and I turn this to us and make sense of it.

Sit back. Relax. There are no appointment times for this. It costs you nothing to spend your free time. You can be in your jammies or wearing a facial mask and read it in a soothing tone to your grandchild.

Remember high school? And then there's the class reunion!

We're so excited to go. "This will be great!" And we all show up differently! With a whole lot of stuff going on between our ears!! And if you're like us, that's 300 plus students with 300 perspectives and 300 experiences. So, let's tackle it...

We had a great time in high school, or we may have had an average high school experience, or maybe we were the class nerd ... by the standards of a high school student, which, of course, is hijacked by the ego.

We graduate, and we're out to tackle the world. It's all of a sudden, our 5-year class reunion, and we're thrilled to be returning. We miss our friends! We want to see where everyone is and how they are all doing. Who has kids? Who does not? Who lives where?

So, we show up looking good. We can't wait to see our buddies. Our ID should be showing up big time! We are walking in with our egos present and in rare form, but it's not that important. Today, the kids might not even go because there's Facebook and for those that participate… they may know all this stuff already. For many of us… we stay off the grid; it's perfect, and it matters. This is 3 dimensional. This is real. This is uninterrupted banter, and we can act like kids. Do we go back to the age of 7? Probably not. What do they look like? Who's gained weight? Who's graduated? Who lives where? People bring their significant others. Boyfriends. New friends. It's fun. Simple. General catch-up. That's 5 years.

10 Years. Now, here we go. We're 28 years old. We have a story to tell.

1. Are we where we thought we would be?

2. Has our story gotten better (more interesting) or less interesting than at the 5-year mark?

3. Was High School so great – we had to revisit it to ensure our legacy?

Another aspect of how others perceive us is our sustainability, which is our aspiration for success. This is the part of ourselves that is aware of where we want to be seen. The places we go tell a story about who we are to other people and reveal the things that we value. Much of this will be subconsciously chosen, but some of it will be on purpose for our presentation to be supported.

This could look like careful budgeting to go to a fancy gym instead of the cheaper economy gym to be seen there or going to get an after-work appetizer and cocktail at a 4-star place instead of a less-known 1-star place. It could be reflected in where we hang out, where we buy clothes, and where we spend our free time. We will look around you and see what is praised or thought well of in society or by the people whose opinions we care about and adjust accordingly. This is, again, normal behavior during this time in our lives. Many people (and maybe even you as you read this now) may pause and realize that some of these habits we built in our twenties are still in place today. We may want to make a conscious effort to outgrow caring so much about "where" we are seen and focus instead on other things we value now.

The final part of our presentation during this age is the direction we are going and receiving personal clarity regarding relationships. This is, very simply with whom we want to be seen. We have enough awareness at this point in our lives that we know who we spend time with and go out with matters, be it at work, at church, around town, or around our family. The person we date says a lot about us and the people we go out to dinner with do as well.

We are also aware of our social value when others ask us to go out or when certain people at work ask us to have lunch with their group. It can impact our own perceived value and can either add to or detract from the presentation we want to give to the world.

Look at the three parts of our presentation and ask yourself if these patterns are still serving you where you are in life now. If they are then great, you made wise decisions in your twenties when these pieces were being put into place. If not, then carefully consider the small and lasting changes you may want to make in your interactions within your mind and with others.

Again, at age of twenty-five the final bits of childhood fall away as our mind finally matures. Each part of our life during this time will challenge and support our ID, Ego, and SuperEgo. We will settle into who we are and carry that foundation with us for the rest of our lives unless we stop and question it, tweaking it along the way. Things we were taught that mattered (finances, education, marriage, the role of family, etc.) are now seen and questioned with adult eyes as we find our autonomy.

Let's take a look at some of the common ideas and terms that meant one thing to us under the influence of our parents and in our child's mind and then see how those words have new meanings or expanded meanings to us, now. The implications and the impacts will have changed quite a bit for many of us, but for some, the meaning may remain largely the same. There is no right or wrong answer to the below activity. Merely, this is a moment to sit quietly and ponder your answers and embrace the truth of each one.

Here is a short Q/A to elaborate on your mindset as your **How** began during your twenties?

How did you feel about money?

_____

_____

_____

How did you feel about your education?

_____

_____

_____

How did you feel about your job?

_____

_____

_____

How did you feel about your life?

_____

_____

_____

How did you feel about your relationships (romance)?

_____

_____

_____

How did you feel about your family?

_____

_____

_____

How did you feel about authority?

_____

_____

_____

If old enough (thirties, forties, fifties, etc.), are your answers of today the same as they were during your twenties?

CHAPTER 6

When – Navigating your Opportunities

"It takes courage to grow up and become who you really are." E.E. Cummings

A kaleidoscope, what a perfect analogy. We know why. We know who. We know what. We know how. The last piece to this complicated prism is the when. This includes our relationships and the opportunities that blossom because of these relationships. The best relationships are built on honesty. And as we can start to see by now, it is when people accept their Communication Temperament (a true balance/understanding of the big three: Why, Who, and What) that inner peace can flourish. As we have experienced, it takes courage to grow up and become who you really are. The human condition of "need to know" versus "not knowing" translates directly into truth, the truth of us, others, and the many patterns each of us has.

Our life evolves by a combination of our choices and our circumstances. We can start to observe and understand the reasons behind our choices and how our circumstances impact those. We might notice our choices are different depending on who we are around or where our body's energy levels are at that moment. This is normal and is not something to judge ourselves for, but rather to acknowledge and adjust as needed. Each new variable (person, place, thing or idea) creates opportunities that are connected to or dependent upon our Communication Temperament (**21T**).

Many of us may see patterns of thinking, speaking, and acting that come out of us seemingly of our own accord. This is a pattern we've created over the decades as we moved through life from a baby up to being an adult. Have you ever heard the saying, "You can't get out of your own way"? It might feel like this sometimes, and hopefully, you've come to understand a little better how we develop as humans and why this saying holds so much accuracy for each of us. We each cherish our thoughts and opinions, actions and reactions, our **21T**. Each of us is an individual before we are anything else. And that is a wonderful thing to consider.

For some, our Communication Temperament may be a hard pill to swallow. Still, it is so valuable to understand it and to continue to observe ourselves in a variety of social and family situations. The more we accept the truth of our why, who, and what, the closer to peace and contentment we become, and the better our connections with others can be. Many people walk around in a daze because they have not taken the time to observe and understand themselves. To recap, our ID (identity) plus our Ego (self-esteem) plus our SuperEgo (self-confidence) equals our Communication Temperament (**21T**).

Living in the Present

Let's dwell a little longer on communication. Every day we interact with our fellow human beings, sometimes in close relationships with them (family units, friends) and sometimes not (work colleagues, neighbors). But in every interaction, our capacity for opportunity can expand or contract depending on how our **21T** interacts with theirs.

When communicating, the key is to slow down. It can be so easy to find words to quickly respond to others, often even cutting them off and not listening. But when we keep our energy (Communication Temperament) in check, this equals respect which is a direct act of love. This type of respect and love is important to give to all humankind. By controlling our **21T**, we will inherently be listening and asking questions to understand the other person fully. Understandably, this can be extremely difficult because of a person's natural tendencies. And it is a great thing that we have seen up to this point how our tendencies can develop and grow stronger over the course of our lives. We are not suggesting that you are poor communicator if listening and speaking slowly is hard for you. Rather, we each can benefit from meeting in the middle and finding a balance that will help us to connect with others.

Balance is a big part of our lives. And the more that is put on our plate, either by ourselves or by others, the more we need to strive to be ourselves. This balancing act can be an extremely positive or negative experience depending upon how it impacts our **21T**. Be patient with yourself during this process.

The difficulty with who we are is that everyone has the same definition of peace (no obstacles) and different definitions based on their Communication Temperament. Here are two quotes to consider when managing your Communication Temperament: "Money can't buy happiness – but peace can," [rjn] and "Love can live in poverty, but the pursuit of happiness can't." [rjn]

Stuck in Neutral

Ever felt like you were carrying the load for your family, at work, etc.? It can feel like you were performing 80% to 100% of the duties needed while another person was overwhelmed by their thoughts and not performing to your expectation.

One way to avoid mishandling this is to observe yourself and see if you are trying to control the environment. Sometimes, this type of control is subtle and not obvious. When you leverage yourself (try to control the environment) to avoid the other person's feelings, it puts the greater good in jeopardy. Isn't it much better to be forthcoming and honest in your communication? We see the opposite of kind communication and keeping our temperament in check a lot in politics, at work, or in family dynamics. One person will not relent to another and tries to do it all themselves or becomes disingenuous. If we instead listen with our **21T** in check, we're hearing what the other person is saying and digesting it. In turn, the result is understanding which puts us in a place of having a more intellectual, open-minded conversation. But if we can't keep our **21T** in check, things can escalate quickly without room for understanding.

It's a journey, and it's work. Good work. Remember I'm the oldest of six kids - I think I've driven that point home – and I now see more clearly how asking and expecting everything, never worrying how that may affect my brothers and sister was pretty darn selfish. If I wanted a new outfit, I got it. My mom's **21T** was all about pleasing people and I unknowingly took full advantage of that.

Let's piece this together... November birth date. Oldest child. Name Patricia. The number 5. Liked everyone and everyone liked me, and my trajectory was moving up and out. So, at 21 when I met my husband, all I could see was continued success! We were in summer school, and he was the greatest thing since sliced bread. He was also the oldest child in his family, the mascot at our university and we were going to "rule the world" with our energy. We got married, life was grand, and everything was funny because he was funny. He made fun of me, always. That's what makes us laugh... when someone hits a chord, right? I was idealistic because I didn't have to be anything else. I was all in.

I eventually learned through his mother and *his* memories of his childhood, how *he* grew up, and what *his* expectations were for *his* adult life – giving me a clearer understanding of *my* **21T**. Marriage is a partnership, so listening is the key. Really listening. After all, he had lived 22 years before we met so my "lollipops and roses" mindset needed to be kept in check and I had to get to work. Today I control my **21T** as much as I can, and we continue to connect using the questions, activities, and information we are sharing in this workbook. I see and understand my husband and our life together differently than ever before.

Manage your Temperament

If we cannot keep our Communication Temperament (**21T**) in check long enough to be open-minded to others, this will eventually create a void in our lives. Our human condition (the need to know vs. not knowing) might try to dictate us not to communicate past our perspective. The human condition is what drives us as we make decisions. This limited perspective is natural to us and is one way our mind keeps itself safe. If we only hear our voices and reinforce our thoughts, our identity of who we are feels secure, and our Ego feels safe. However, that centripetal force that we so crave to feel can't survive in this type of mindset. If we can't get out of the way to acquire it because of our own **21T**, most of our relationships will feel shallow or volatile. This may transform into a building up of resentment, baggage, and hurt.

This creates a singular focus and restricts us from experiencing happiness/joy/contentment unless things go our way.

When was the last time you heard yourself in an argument or a debate? If you have, chances are you might be wondering who that person is. Often, our pride steps up to the plate to try for a home run against the other person when communicating. This means we listen just enough to respond quickly instead of taking time and holding our emotions in check. It isn't easy to mature this way, but the results will be well worth it.

Prioritize

Time is both an abundant and limited resource as well as the measurement of our past. When discussions become tense, we look to the past for advice, clues, or evidence that will support our stance or perspective. This is in relationships and in every part of life. Do you ever feel in your relationships, using the past or the history of the person against them is hurtful and not productive? But taking a moment to reflect on our past shortcomings can be helpful when seeking the truth. We touched upon how it can feel that we are carrying the load for others or how they may think they are carrying it for us. Relationship percentages can be seen in how we balance situations and circumstances. We are indeed individuals first before anything else, and we need relationships in a general sense for our well-being. Mostly likely, we have all intentionally removed relationships in our life to keep peace. *A family member. A childhood friend. A college classmate. A neighbor. A boss.*

One way we can gain the ability to see priorities appropriately is to keep the big picture in mind. The current moment may feel all-consuming, or we may feel fully focused on keeping our **21T** in check, but don't get lost in the weeds at the expense of connection with the other person. The more we can develop our ability to see past the task at hand and see the bigger picture for everyone involved, the more balanced we become.

Take a look at the percentages below and think of your closest relationships as well as your professional relationships. Write down a circumstance/task that falls within each percentage below and determine how you feel about that and what you can do to make it better.

LIFE IS EASY

100/0:

Example: The dog eats 2x per day and yep... she bought him, and I feed him 😊

_____

_____

_____

80/20:

_____

_____

_____

50/50:

Example: Dishes in my marriage... we have got each other's back, but she always makes it known when she has mine 😊

_____

_____

_____

20/80:

_____

_____

_____

0/100:

_____

_____

_____

We may find that with many people each time we are around them, we do most of the heavy lifting, and we fight to keep our emotions in check. Over time, we may start to feel resentful of this or develop a poor attitude. But remember, we cannot control other people or their levels of self-awareness. All we can do is control our attitude, emotions, and reactions. By knowing our Communication Temperament and choosing to take our emotions out of the equation to hear the other person, we are showing them (and ourselves!) respect and love.

A truly profound saying that supports our thoughts on this topic is: "Listen and the world will hear you." This is directly the opposite of how many people live their lives. Still, it is far more powerful to practice the listening we discussed in this chapter than to continue in the patterns most of us have of control and reactivity. This is the beginning of true support. If we stop and think about all  the times we felt supported in our life, many of them are likely when others held space for us through this type of listening. Even if they did not know they were doing so, the result was that we felt supported. Most human beings who lack support will soften their rough edges (we all have those!) through repeated exposure to this type of supportive listening.

Communication Temperament is a complex and powerful topic that can carry some negative connotations at first. We hope you can accept the truth (all three parts) of your Communication Temperament. It is an integral part of who you are, and in many instances in your life, it has served you well and helped you through tough moments. In other instances, you may come to realize it did not serve you well and want to make sure you can rein it in as needed when communicating.

LIFE IS EASY

We hope that you accept the reality that most of the people around us do not yet have the knowledge we have shared in this book and therefore may not succeed in keeping their emotions and **21T** in check. This will burden you to hold back your emotions and see them through patient and understanding eyes.

Through the concepts we are exploring together in each chapter, we hope it gives you renewed purpose, understanding, and direction in life.

"The hardest thing in life is to live without direction." rjn

So, pause now and contemplate, what is important to you? Write about it and be specific. Use the space below to elaborate on the situations or environments when you are the happiest and/or at peace?

At Work/School:

_____

_____

_____

With Family/Friends:

Example: Being around my family but not all at once. We always resort back to yesterday, and I like a little more depth in conversation than volume.

_____

_____

_____

Your Life: This can include your past, present, or future.

_____

_____

_____

_____

CHAPTER 7

Peace and Happiness

As we have journeyed through the chapters, we have come to see why, who, and what we are as it means for ourselves and those around us. One of the driving forces in life for many humans is the constant push, either away from fear or pain, or toward happiness. Let's talk about how to acquire true happiness and peace, understanding that these terms probably have definitions taught to you by family, faith, friends, your **21T**.

We live our lives. We need each other to exist. We experience success, failures, and emotions only seen through our perspective (**21T**) by our decisions. We are here for a relatively short period. Not one of us is greater or lesser than the other. So, let us not waste energy being obligated to false images, thoughts, ideas, and aspirations to validate another person's life. When, in fact, we only have an ever-changing percentage to do with our own life in the first place. Looking at others is a sure way to remove ourselves from happiness and peace.

Remember when we talked about how circumstances control man, then man dictates the outcome, and TIME (**The Internal Mental Evaluation**) is forever our measuring stick? There are a few parts to this: clarity, communication, and the challenge we can give ourselves for the future. Let's start with clarity.

> *"The study of history is a waste of time – a reflection is just fine".* [rjn]

Clarity

After age twenty-one, we believe that a person does not change. The many changes babies and toddlers go through have been completed, and human beings are who they will continue to be. If you feel resistance to this, take some time right now to explore your resistance and come to accept this simple idea. This idea creates a recurring challenge – taking time to see ourselves and others for who we really are. If we have had a tough patch or two in our lives or feel that we are constantly being mistreated or left behind, taking a look at ourselves and others can be a difficult task. But ultimately it will help us to find peace. Running away from the hardships of childhood, or adulthood, only prolongs our suffering. It takes bravery and courage to be honest with ourselves and look within.

Hey, I was the oldest (**we know**). For just a few months the sun rose and set on my schedule. I was a happy, easy baby with good energy. I guess I continued that trek with siblings 2, 3, and 4 in my wake because when I finally got to kindergarten, and I'm sure my mother was relieved on that day, I was a "delight to have in class," and it continued from there. I never considered myself the teacher's pet because I wasn't a kiss-up, but I sure was liked. *You sense it… you know what I mean?* I didn't cause trouble. I did my homework. I asked questions and school was always a positive memory no matter the grade I was in. A little "Marcia Marcia Marcia" if you will? I was trusted. I wasn't ugly. I wasn't mean in the least bit; I had not an enemy. And to me that was life. Being kind and making friends.

50 years later and I'm still bringing energy to a space, to a group of people, to a meeting, *so I'm told.* People feel it. To this day I like to be liked. So why am I in business-to-consumer sales? I didn't mean to be, that's for sure, I intended to help people. Little did I know until I received that 100th "no" everyone brings their **21T** to the table. So now, it's not so easy and my being liked definitely trumps my persistence *even though* I am 100% certain of my product. (And I do my due diligence just like I did my homework.) People don't change. I have to work a lot harder and exercise far greater discipline than I ever thought I'd have to in order to help people. So, I ask myself… "How spoiled am I?" "How driven am I?" And, *wow…* "I'd give everything up just to be trusted, wouldn't I!"

Maybe looking within isn't a matter of pain but something you feel your busy life doesn't allow for. So many of us are busy taking care of others, such as our children or grandchildren, our job responsibilities, and ourselves, that it can be nearly impossible to get a moment to ourselves where we have the time and energy to do the work needed to know ourselves.

Sarah, Robert's daughter, once said, "People don't wait for you to live up to your full potential or your reaction."

Even reading this book is taking up all the time you can offer to yourself for self-discovery and a healing journey. This is a great step in the right direction. Continue to carve out time for this process and feel free to return to any section of this book that you need another moment of focus on.

Looking within and seeing who we are does not have to be scary. Because if we are truly honest about who we are, it's not what we do or did that will make/made a difference – it's who we are as a person that perpetuates the belief within another. Others are reading our body language cues, assessing our words, and interpreting our actions. What is in our psyche will eventually come out, and who we are as human beings can impact those around us. If in our psyche we believe that others usually are not evil people, that will surface in big and small ways.

For example, we say thank you when someone reciprocates our social graces because at that point if we know or we do not know their **21T** we still know that they have made a concerted effort for us which supports a positive belief in mankind.

The reverse can be true, too. We may find ourselves suspicious about the intentions of others, no matter how quickly they reciprocate social graces. This can reveal some of the impressions you received during your young, formative years and how those impressions stayed with you during your teen years, up to age twenty-one, and this day.

Now is a great time to take a moment and reflect. Write one sentence to express/illustrate how you have truly changed (after age twenty-one). This can be any change. Write down the first one that comes to your mind.

_____

_____

_____

Communication

The next topic we want to explore together is communication. We have touched upon many aspects of communication already, but still, there is more! This exciting topic has many layers that impact us and the people in our lives.

First, have you ever heard about the communication tree? This is a great way to see how communication works and the many moving parts of it. In the communication tree, we have four areas of interest within communication. They are the sender, the message itself, the receiver, and the timing of the message.

Think of it this way. You are a teenager coming home after school, and you were just invited to the popular girl's Friday night party. You want to go, but you're pretty sure your mom won't let you go. How do you overcome this obstacle? Communicating with your mom to the best of your ability so that she might consider saying yes. You may start by immediately doing all your chores when you're home, complimenting her, and waiting for the right time when she seems in a good mood before you ask her. You may verbally assure her that there will be parents at the party and that the party is at the schoolmate's home, and that even the local pastor's daughter will be going. Up to this point, you have controlled the sender (yourself), the timing (when you ask), and the message (how you word what you ask for) but the one part you cannot control is, of course, the receiver. It will be completely up to them how your words land into their mind and psyche, and whether they respond favorably or not to you.

The communication tree happens every day with each conversation we have with others. We give information, others hear us, and we move on. But left in our wake is the energy of our communication. Did we communicate, nicely, politely, or impatiently, critically, and dismissively? The communication tree can build upon layer by layer when we have recurring interactions with people. It is important to know our Communication Temperament and how we make others feel during and after communication.

So many of the opportunities in life come from communicating with others. Communication is only about 10% verbal and roughly 90% nonverbal through body language and tone of voice. This nonverbal part is the one that can stay with others in a strong impression for years or decades because it most strongly reveals our Communication Temperament (**21T** – first twenty-one years of life). Just as we don't want others to judge us because we are each still a work in progress and there is more going on with us than what meets the eye, it is important not to judge others, either. The old saying, "Don't judge a book by its cover," holds true today. People are layered and valuable enough for us to take a little time when receiving a message from them before reacting or responding.

Your **21T** may have developed so that you can very easily see the message behind the words of others, so you may be tempted to interrupt or be impatient for others to get to the point. You can certainly do this, but if we want to connect genuinely, it could be more positive to hold back our tendencies to allow others a little room to be themselves.

Along these lines is the need for us to see others as special and unique individuals rather than making snap judgments about them. For those who rub us the wrong way or have harmed us, this can trigger some feelings within us of doubt or even fear. But by trying to give others the freedom to stand on their merit and offering forgiveness for past wrongs, we can often overcome our doubts or fears about them or things they may have said or done in the past.

Does forgiveness make the heart grow lighter?

Indeed, you don't change after age twenty-one, but you can effectively communicate and become part of a solution. It takes a willingness to absorb another point of view by keeping your point of view in check. This is a hard thing to accomplish. Imagine that through this journey of self-awareness it will be possible to get there! You will find your life is more peaceful and others are drawn to your confidence and acceptance. You can reach a point where you can appreciate a point of view as neither being right nor wrong, but just human. From there you can peacefully concede that all men are indeed created equal. When we hold so tightly to one perspective it tends to elevate our minds as being right, and therefore puts others down as less than, which is not healthy or true.

While others are staunchly holding on to their beliefs and you are systematically listening better and with kindness, it will feel like you are giving others a gift. And really, it is more than that. It is an invitation for them to become self-aware, as you have. This gift can be built out into a strong love for humanity, one of the greatest gifts you can offer to the world. Out of this love is true communication, speaking truth with kindness and speaking in our truth. It is more than compassionate speak, which often comes with its strings and expectations; thinking "I gave you this, and now you owe me." Doesn't it seem to be more authentic to embrace truth than to enslave others through this type of rhetoric?

"A million plays of compassion are humbled by one act of truth." rjn

To recap, we are how we communicate, and this comes through in our **21T**, our own unique, one-of-a-kind as an individual, way of communicating with others. Admittedly, this special Communication Temperament that we have can be expressed well and can be expressed poorly. We all have excellent moments of good communication and we all have the opposite.

Write a sentence to describe what it is like when you are communicating at your best and then write a sentence to describe what it is like when you are communicating at your worst.

Example: When I am in a big picture conversation and everything is clicking into place, I feel like I can speak clearly and my mind feels free. But then if I get pulled into the weeds, I instantly get indifferent – annoyed with what I interpret as another person using community orientation to manipulate outcomes.

_____

_____

_____

It is easy to see how our Communication Temperament can be triggered based on our mentality toward what is happening around us as well as our reactions to others' Communication Temperament.

Challenge

As we understand ourselves and come to appreciate who we are, we unlock the capacity to understand the power of one, of "me" as an individual. It is the second part of the upcoming passage that seems to be the most important and can signify where we can derive strength. Interestingly, there is only one number associated with it–the number one. This represents a single entity—you. Our hope with this exercise is to help you see things a little broader and the power of free will. Please read the following message.

(Blank) give me the Grace to accept with serenity the things that cannot be changed, Courage to change the things which should be changed, and the Wisdom to distinguish the one from the other.

Living one day at a time, Enjoying one moment at a time, Accepting hardship as a pathway to peace, Taking, as Jesus did, this sinful world as it is, Not as I would have it, Trusting that *(blank)* will make things right, If I surrender to *(blank)* will, So that I may be reasonably happy in this life, And supremely happy with *(blank)* forever in the next.

Did you fill in the blanks with a person, place, thing, or an idea? If so, ask yourself why?

You may not have yet discovered or heard of the term "free will." This is what free will is—unlocking the power of who you are (by your spirit and truth) to set and manage expectations. The phrase "the truth will set you free" means that the truth gives us freedom from self. Rather than walk through life enslaved to patterns of behavior, the truth lets us consciously decide who to be and what to do. It happens a bit at a time that we can let go of ourselves from patterns and walk into free will. This slow and organic process equals grace. And with grace, we can exercise free will in all parts of our lives.

As we have discussed throughout the book and now acknowledge again, self-awareness (spirit) and self-acceptance (truth) are the two pieces that echo our Communication Temperament. A temperament now referred to as your own **21T**. A tremendous gift, yes, but not the ultimate gift we hope it to be. The real present is to manage this **21T**, a guide first bestowed on a mountain by ten simple decrees. Without judgment, self-validation, or the bullying nature of compassion – Oh, how easy life could be, if we just support and believe in one another instead of thee.

Write one sentence on how you are going to challenge yourself going forward. There are no right or wrong answers, we ask that you speak your truth.

_____

_____

_____

LIFE IS EASY

The Wrap Up

We are all individuals first before we are anything else. Our lives are the sum total of all our circumstances, events, and decisions made. We are creatures of habit and our Communication Temperament (**21T**) does not change after the age of twenty-one.

Whatever you became after twenty-one, here is the good news! When you become self-aware (your spirit) and self-accepting (your truth) – you can deliver true support (the belief) in another without judgment, self-validation, or the bullying nature of compassion to make life easy.

Do you tell the truth with clarity? Do you listen to understand? Do you keep your **21T** in check?

Free the past, present, and future you!

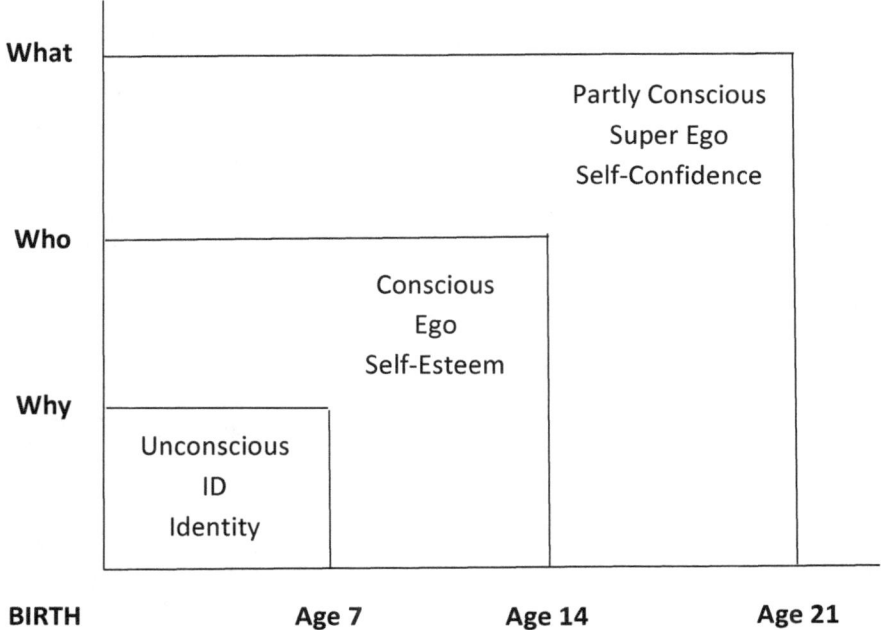

References

Chapter 2

Goldschneider, G (2005). Personology: The Precision Approach to charting your life, career, and relationships. Running Press

Auntyflo.com (2020)

Leman, Dr. K (2015). The Birth Order Book: Why you are the way you are. Revell, A division of Baker Publishing Group

Chapter 7

Niebuhr, R (1932). Serenity Prayer

www.ingramcontent.com/pod-product-compliance
Lightning Source LLC
Chambersburg PA
CBHW081432070526
44586CB00020B/2555